Conversations Around Semiotic Engineering

Simone Diniz Junqueira Barbosa • Karin Breitman
Editors

Conversations Around Semiotic Engineering

Springer

Editors
Simone Diniz Junqueira Barbosa
Departamento de Informática
PUC-Rio
Rio de Janeiro, Brazil

Karin Breitman
Corporate VP & GM Brazil Labs
Dell EMC | Services
Rio de Janeiro, Brazil

ISBN 978-3-319-56290-2 ISBN 978-3-319-56291-9 (eBook)
DOI 10.1007/978-3-319-56291-9

Library of Congress Control Number: 2017937752

Printed on acid-free paper

This Springer imprint is published by Springer Nature
The registered company is Springer International Publishing AG
The registered company address is: Gewerbestrasse 11, 6330 Cham, Switzerland

Preface

It is our great pleasure to introduce this tribute to Clarisse Sieckenius de Souza's research. When Clarisse established the Semiotic Engineering Research Group (SERG), in 1996, she managed to bring together not only her own students but also students from other areas who were inspired by her unique ideas and rigorous reasoning.

We feel privileged to have been there in its inception and to have followed semiotic engineering's evolution. It started as a theory of human-computer interaction (HCI), with a particular view of HCI as designer-to-user metacommunication, thus typifying HCI as a kind of computer-mediated communication (de Souza 2005). Later, semiotic engineering proposed to use some of its evaluation methods in scientific research in HCI (de Souza & Leitão, 2009) and, more recently, a set of epistemic tools to inform human-centered computing (de Souza et al. 2016).

In this volume, several researchers who have in some way been touched by or contributed to Clarisse's work have come together to participate in a range of conversations around semiotic engineering, each from their own unique perspective.

Terry Winograd opens the volume recollecting Clarisse's time as a visitor researcher at Stanford. Their vibrant research environment inspired her to explore her intuitions about bringing the HCI designers to the center stage as interlocutors of a semiotic conversation. That visit provided a fertile soil in which Clarisse planted the first seeds of semiotic engineering.

By situating semiotic engineering as one of the few "more general conceptual approaches," Liam Bannon highlights the theoretical and ethical commitments of semiotic engineering in the design of technologies that augment humans' skills and expertise.

Susanne Bødker brings attention to the need to explore the role of multimediation, meaning, and appropriation in ubiquitous settings, with their multiplicity of artifacts and activities. Her multi-mediation work with Peter Bøgh Andersen and other colleagues, combining semiotics with activity theory, shares with semiotic engineering a concern for designing technology oriented toward people mediated by multiple (interactive, computational) artifacts.

Sharing an interest in creating “richer frameworks and ecologies on how designers and users can interact in the design of computational artifacts,” Gerhard Fischer proposes to establish an alliance between semiotic engineering and his own work in meta-design, to face the challenge of embracing the emergent “and making it an opportunity for more creative and more adequate solutions to problems.”

In the domain of programming languages, Alan Blackwell argues for a shift in focus from language designers (“the last people to listen to”) to programmers (i.e., the language users). From a semiotic engineering standpoint, this may be viewed as going from one extreme to another, as semiotic engineering proposes to bring designers to the center stage as interlocutors with equal standing as users.

Delving into oft-misunderstood concepts of semiotics, Mihai Nadin recalls his argument in favor of a new foundation for semiotics and proposes a discussion about semiotic engineering’s role in designing effective interaction languages that reach the pragmatic level of semiotics.

Allen Cypher draws a parallel between some of the characteristics semiotic engineering leverages in designers and characteristics of good teachers, such as “the ability to go a step further and imagine what it will be like for their audience to hear those words.” Thinking of the audience in a different way, within computational arts, Ernest Edmonds continues a conversation started in 2015, in Rio, after Clarisse and he met in a computer-based art exhibit. The debate about the “locus” of conception of generative art and its relation to semiotic engineering is wide-ranging, thought provoking, and far from over.

Diving into semiotic engineering, Raquel Prates discusses its advances in the creation of epistemic tools for the design of collaborative systems over the years, framing them as members of the EpisTAMiCS family of models, each one addressing complementary parts of the design process that help to reflect on design alternatives and to make better informed design decisions.

Carla Leitão concludes this book, charting the trajectory of semiotic engineering from its inception onto a reflexive, transdisciplinary, and humanistic theory, which started within HCI but which has now moved beyond, reaching into human-centered computing (HCC) with a set of epistemic tools for various “users” in multiple stages in software development, such as engineers and programmers.

The breadth of conversation topics inspired by semiotic engineering demonstrates the range of influence of the theory and the relevance of Clarisse’s lifework to diverse scientific and artistic realms. We hope our readers will also feel inspired to engage in some of these conversations.

Rio de Janeiro, Brazil

Simone Diniz Junqueira Barbosa
Karin Breitman

References

De Souza CS (2005) The semiotic engineering of human-computer interaction. The MIT Press.
De Souza CS, Leitão CF (2009) Semiotic engineering methods for scientific research in HCI. Morgan and Claypool.
De Souza CS, Cerqueira RFG, Afonso LM, Brandão RFM, Ferreira JJ (2016) Software developers as users. Semiotic investigations in human-centered software Development. Springer.

Contents

About the Editors

Simone Diniz Junqueira Barbosa is associate professor at the Informatics Department of the Pontifical Catholic University of Rio de Janeiro (PUC-Rio), where she teaches, advises, and conducts research in the field of Human-Computer Interaction (HCI).

Dr. Karin Breitman is a Vice President at Dell EMC and currently serves as the chief-scientist of the Brazil Labs. Her research focuses on Software Engineering and their applications to Knowledge Representation, Data Science, and Cloud Computing.

Clarisse's Visit at CSLI Stanford, 1991–1992

Terry Winograd

Abstract Clarisse spent several months as a visiting researcher at the Center for the Study of Language and Information (CSLI) at Stanford in 1991–1992. In this chapter, I briefly recount the context of our work at Stanford during that time and relate it with Clarisse's own research interests. She recognized that help systems are not operating in a world of information, but as part of a semiotic conversation. I believe her visit at CSLI and her discussions with our research group played a role the genesis of her work in semiotic engineering.

I had the pleasure of getting to work with Clarisse in 1991–1992 when she spent several months as a visiting researcher at the Center for the Study of Language and Information (CSLI) at Stanford.

At the time, I had a small group of students working on new technologies for unifying information on the Internet. As context, it is important to remember that this was when the World Wide Web was just a fledgling project at CERN, used by physicists. It was only in 1991 that it was opened to anyone outside of CERN, and the first server outside Europe was installed that year at the Stanford Linear Accelerator Center (SLAC) to host the SPIRES-HEP database. Nobody (including Tim Berners Lee) envisioned what the web would later become as a universal medium for information, communication, and commerce. The first browser (line mode) wasn't until 1992, and the graphical browser (Mosaic) wouldn't come along for more than another year.

There were already a growing number of Internet hosts, reaching a few hundred thousand (compared to more than a billion today). The unifying interface (to the extent there was one) was the IETF protocols for textual interaction (TELNET) and file transfer (FTP). These in turn were being made more "user friendly" through clients such as WAIS, Gopher, and Fetch, which allowed users to avoid the arcane user interaction of the underlying protocols. The model was one of repositories – one host had files of interest in its file system, and someone on another host could transfer them to another computer. The first primitive search was just coming into place.

T. Winograd (✉)
Stanford University, Stanford, CA 94305, USA
e-mail: winograd@cs.stanford.edu

S.D.J. Barbosa, K. Breitman (eds.), *Conversations Around Semiotic Engineering*, DOI 10.1007/978-3-319-56291-9_1

In this fragmented environment, we set out to create a client interface that could retrieve, organize, and store information in a way that was higher level than file systems and Internet protocols. We programmed the system on NeXT machines, which at the time seemed to be a window into the future. The (at the time novel) object-oriented development tools and libraries gave us leverage to provide users with uniform and understandable access to a wide diversity of native formats and protocols.

This project never led to deployable software, as it was overtaken by the sweep of events, including the growth of Web browsers (which provided a uniform interface, although not for a while) and the demise of NeXT. The work was one of the starting points for the Stanford Digital Libraries project, which also dealt with the cacophony of materials on the Internet, just before the web took hold. One project we initiated within the Digital Libraries Project later developed into Google, which brought a new scale and unity to web search.

But we're getting ahead of the story. At the time Clarisse was at Stanford, we were still at the stage of creating interfaces to diverse materials and protocols. She got interested in looking at help systems in a more general way. There were individual help systems for different operating systems and applications, which were primitive by today's standards. Online help only existed in the form of bulletin boards. The help systems dealt with specific commands, not with tasks or the application's underlying conceptual model, which the user needed to understand.

The first level of thinking was how to integrate immediate help, help texts, and online interactive help in a unified system. This would include the potential for question asking, and also could serve as a feedback loop for designers to understand the problems that users encountered.

Clarisse took a deeper view, asking about the nature of help systems and system learning. She recognized that help systems are not operating in a world of information, but as part of a semiotic conversation. Her key insight was that by their very nature, software artifacts are meta-communication artifacts – they communicate about communication. HCI is a two-tiered communicative process: the obvious one is the communication between user and system, which we think of as the "interface". But behind it there is communication between the designer and the user, about the nature and possibilities that the system is intended to provide.

From a semiotic perspective, we need to look at both the direct and indirect messages from designers that are embodied in the software. We also need to look for the intent that drives users in their use of the system (both the basic system and the help system around it). By directly dealing with communicative intent, we can provide help of a much more fundamental kind than the simple "tool tip" explanations of interface features. Online help systems are a privileged communication channel for designers to tell users all about the application they have developed.

This approach was later articulated in her paper Semiotic Engineering Contributions for Designing Online Help Systems (Silveira et al. 2001). In that paper, the authors describe a methodology for designers to apply the semiotic insights to the software they are designing. They point out that in addition to obvious questions, such as "What does this do?" the user has deeper questions, such as "What else should I know? And "Why should I use this program?" By getting designers to address the meta-communication issues directly, they can address user-intent sensitivity issues focusing on what the help component can or should be sensitive to or independent of in various user-intent scenarios.

In the field of practical software development, there is a quest for structured methods, checklists, and tools that the designer and programmer can employ to make the software have desirable properties. For superficial aspects, such as menu consistency, this works well. But for deeper issues, it is often not possible to provide "canned" lists, guidelines, and procedures. This is an issue I encountered in my own work on a phenomenological approach to software (Winograd and Flores 1986). There is no ("phenomenological checklist") that can be applied in a systematic way. The impact on the design is effected not through particular methods, but through a shift in perspective that leads the designer to look at different aspects and ask new questions that then have an impact on the design.

Semiotics, like phenomenology, is what I call an "orienting theory" (Winograd 2006). This is a distinction from other kinds (and ambitions for) theories. The most common use of the word "theory" is for formal predictive theories, of the kind that dominate physics and the natural sciences. From Newton on, we look for theories that can be expressed in formal mathematical terms, and from which we can derive precise predications about what will happen. As is now becoming more clear when we consider complex natural phenomena, such as global warming, this ideal of a predictive theory cannot be met, even for natural physical systems, but it still dominates the public and professional conversation.

A second kind is what I call an empirical descriptive theory. As with predictive theories, it takes a perspective outside the phenomena it is describing, using observation, data, statistical inference, and other tools to make sense of what is being observed. Most of what is called theory in the social sciences is of this kind.

The third kind, orienting theory, does not take the observer's view of existing phenomena, but provides a foundation for creating new phenomena, whether they be linguistic utterances, software, or equipment. It does not offer a method for determining what will happen, but *poses a set of questions that orient the creator* (designer) to concerns of the different groups of people who are affected by the *design*. Both phenomenology and semiotics are theories of this kind, which are of critical importance in the design of human systems.

Semiotic Engineering, as described in Clarisse's book, *The Semiotic Engineering of Human-Computer Interaction*, is most valuable as an approach to what questions the designer should be asking. In their experiments with student designers, Clarisse and her colleagues observed how the semiotic engineering approach led them to reflect for the first time about underlying important issues, which then led to changes in the applications' conception itself. This has applicability far beyond the classroom, as the phenomena of semiotic conversation with the user pervades every computer system that has humans anywhere "in the loop".

I am proud to believe that the early experience Clarisse had in working with our research group played a role in the development of her semiotic theory. They will continue to be the basis for new productive thinking in the future, by her, by her colleagues and students, and by the larger HCI community.

References

De Souza CS (2005) The semiotic engineering of human-computer interaction. MIT press
Silveira MS, de Souza CS, Barbosa, SDJ (2001) Semiotic engineering contributions for designing online help systems. In: Proceedings of the 19th annual international conference on computer documentation, SIGDOC 2001
Winograd T (2006) Designing a new foundation for design. Commun ACM 49(5):71–74
Winograd T, Flores F (1986) Understanding computers and cognition. Addison-Wesley, New York

Elucidating Frames of Reference for HCI

Liam J. Bannon

Abstract This essay briefly outlines the historical and intellectual development of the HCI field. It notes the shift from the early study of machine operators in industrial human factors to the study of blue and white-collar workers using computer-based systems to accomplish their work tasks. As computer-based systems became ubiquitous in the workplace, the need for the development of easy-to-use interfaces to these systems grew, leading to the creation of the human-computer interaction (HCI) field. The view of the human as an information processor dominated the early days of HCI, but over time other conceptual frameworks were explored. One view of the computer was as an intelligent agent – the AI approach, another focused on human-computer-human interaction, where the computer is viewed as a medium. This latter view, a semiotic perspective, has been developed, under the rubric of Semiotic Engineering by the Brazilian linguist and HCI researcher, Clarisse Sieckenius de Souza. The spread of this conceptual framework may lead to the development of a more truly 'human-centred' computing discipline.

Early HCI – The Human Information-Processing Perspective

The field of HCI emerged in the early 1980's. The emergence of the field was a result of the confluence of a number of challenges in the computing sector. As computer-based systems became more widespread in both factories and offices, the traditional area of human factors – associated with the study of human operators of machinery – enlarged to deal with the heterogeneous and diverse range of new computer 'users', whose primary focus was not on operating the computer *per se*, but in accomplishing their work tasks through computer-based systems. The human performance engineering perspective of many of these human factors personnel seemed ill equipped to deal with the shift in human-machine interaction from a physical to

---

L.J. Bannon (✉)
University of Limerick, Limerick, Ireland

Aarhus University, Aarhus, Denmark
e-mail: liam.bannon@ul.ie

S.D.J. Barbosa, K. Breitman (eds.), *Conversations Around Semiotic Engineering*, DOI 10.1007/978-3-319-56291-9_2

a more cognitively based ergonomics. More extensive "communication" facilities were required between humans and systems. As the field broadened, and searched for new perspectives, many cognitive psychologists became involved, along with some software engineers interested in the usability of their computer-based systems. At the time, the dominant paradigm in the emerging discipline of what was termed 'human-computer interaction' was that of human information processing – viewing the human mind as akin to a computer. The person was seen as someone who "processes" information, through receiving "inputs" through sensory channels, then performs some operations in a central processing unit, interacting with a "memory" thus producing an "output" via the motor system. This model of human functioning was of course influenced by the rise of the computer, with its CPU, Memory and I/O channels.

For many cognitive psychologists, the growth of interest in human-machine systems opened up new sources of research funding and new opportunities. Many general problems in the field of cognitive psychology could be re-fashioned into an applied cognitive psychology – concerned with human-machine "communication". Underlying much of this work was the notion that an ideal interface between a machine and a person would be a simulated human that acted as an interlocutor at the computer interface. Thus, many accepted the notion that human-machine communication should attempt to duplicate human-human communication. Crucially however, this notion can be interpreted in radically different ways. One way, the road most travelled at the time, was to assume that we should make our computer systems behave as if they were intelligent – i.e. that they should interact with their human operator in quasi-natural language, perhaps even with a level of connected speech understanding. Thus, a huge amount of research went into attempting to make human-computer interaction mimic human-human interaction. As many of the senior cognitive psychologists at the time were also enamoured of the potential of artificial intelligence, and with the strong overlap of the models of human and computer that they held, large programmes in AI-type machine interfaces that simulated human performance were funded. By the 1990's the results from this approach were coming in, and they were not promising. It turned out that making computers simulate human intelligence and especially everyday reasoning was difficult. Also, the complexities of human communication became more apparent. Attempting to mimic human-human interaction turned out to be problematic. Conversation analysts, many coming from an ethnomethodological perspective, showed how human conversation was intimately tied to human practices in the world, and depended on human embodiment in the physical world. Treating machine agents as if they were real human beings led to many insurmountable problems. The overly mentalistic conceptions of mind as being similar to a disembodied computer came home to roost.

Towards Human-Computer-Human Interaction

There was yet another perspective emerging on human-computer interaction in these early years, which, however, did not get much airplay at the time, or even for many years subsequently. This was one that viewed human computer interaction as in reality better described as *human (designer)-computer-human (user) interaction*. In other words, rather than thinking that the person is operating on, or communicating with, the machine, whether through language or by direct manipulation, this alternative viewpoint views the computer software as being the construction of a human software designer, who creates an artifact, the computer application, as a vehicle for their communication with the user of the system. In this approach, HCI is fundamentally a linguistic, or more correctly, a semiotic act between human actors, not between a human user and the machine *per se*. Taking such an approach requires us to radically re-think what is going on when we write software, and indeed extends beyond simply how we view the "interface". The computer system acts as a mediator between the designer and the user. Designers express themselves through signs in the interface – buttons, text boxes, etc., and their associated actions, through the writing of programmes, or scripts, for their behavior under specified conditions. It is this approach that has been pursued over many years by the Brazilian linguist and HCI researcher Clarisse Sieckenius de Souza.

As de Souza (2012) notes, in an excellent introductory essay on Semiotics and HCI, a semiotic approach to computing and computer interfaces has been discussed by a small number of researchers over the years. De Souza specifically references the early work of Mihai Nadin (1988) and the more extensive work of the Danish linguist Peter Bøgh Andersen (1990). In the area of computer art, another pioneer of a semiotic approach was the German computer scientist and artist, Frieder Nake. All have discussed how a semiotic approach can provide an illuminating perspective on the nature of human-computer interfaces and on the whole domain of computing. Computers are viewed as carriers of signs, thus a form of media. However, what distinguishes the work of de Souza is the detailed and systematic way in which she and her team have developed, over the years, an "engineering" approach to actually showing how this semiotic perspective on systems design and use can be developed, through the use of numerous techniques and methods that can be learned and applied systematically. This complex of theory, method, and practice, evolved over many years, and has been labeled by de Souza as the "Semiotic Engineering" perspective.

In my own journey through the HCI field over the years, I too have at times been disappointed with the mainstream information-processing view on HCI, and have searched for alternatives. Viewing the computer as a medium through which we communicate, and thus looking for inspiration at how we analyse other media, was one way of attempting to re-position the field, although this lacked a clear conceptual frame (Bannon 1986a). Focusing on human activity and the way technology mediates our activities in the world was another viewpoint. This approach, linking to the ideas of Soviet psychologists Vygotsky and later Leontjev (Bannon and

Bødker 1991; Bannon and Kaptelinin 2000) again repositioned the computer as a system through which we act on the world, as elucidated by Susanne Bødker (1989). The pioneering work of Winograd and Flores (1986) on Language as Action helped us in rethinking the whole ontology and epistemology of Computing, and HCI. What many of these approaches emphasized was the importance of human *meaning-making* and *interpretation* in making sense of our activities with and through technology. Tools and language are *mediators* in our everyday life. It is here where the influence of semiotics – the study of signs and their meaning – becomes central. We can view computers as semiotic machines. They manipulate signs. The signs are given meaning through a process of interpretation, which is done by people. (More correctly, machines themselves only deal directly with signals, not signs, as the meaning making is done by humans, not the computer *per se*). Also, signs and their meaning are constantly undergoing change – *ongoing semiosis* – through use, among a community. So it is not enough to look at single users, we must look at a community of users and the cultural setting, thus opening up further avenues for observation and research explorations.

In terms of HCI, while researchers began to pay more attention to the use situation, and to the work context, there was still a tendency to see the computer program or application as something fixed, with its behavior pre-determined by the system designers at design time. The focus was on designing the behavior of the artifact, rather than on engaging in a communicative process with the end user. One of the interesting openings provided by de Souza in her work on Semiotic Engineering is to expand the discourse in HCI to include examining the role of the design team, the choices they make, and the meanings they assign to various computer signs, together with attention to how these designed signs might be understood by their users. de Souza argues that this has been neglected in much HCI work to date, even in the work under the rubric of user-centred design. She notes: "The problem of UCD … is that it cannot accommodate computer-mediated communication between systems designers and users. Designers, quite plainly, do not belong in UCD interaction models" (de Souza 2012). I feel this is perhaps overly strong, as there is a sense in the early cognitive engineering HCI literature where the designer is mentioned, but their input is seen as being "fixed" in the programme, and system features and documentation of the system, which then are accessed by the user – what Norman (1986) refers to as the "system image". So there is, in this UCD approach some limited sense of thinking about computer applications in terms of how the "system image" reflects the designer's intent, and how it is interpreted by the users. However, it is certainly the case that this falls far short of what de Souza is proposing, in terms of making the designer's sign-making processes embodied in the programme and the interface an integral part of the HCI frame.

de Souza's proposal for a Semiotic Engineering approach is evocative and engaging, as she is mixing aspects of the linguistic and semiotic traditions of Saussure and Peirce on signification systems and meaning making with an "engineering" approach, in terms of developing methods and techniques on how exactly to study these issues and influence not just our understanding of computer use, but the very *design* of computer systems. Understanding aspects of designer-user communication in terms of a *metacommunication* process, and examining the *communicability* of the system are thus new issues that emerge for the HCI field with this approach.

Today, much of the HCI field is dominated by more practical usability concerns, with a relative paucity of more sustained conceptual efforts. For many in the field, more general conceptual approaches, such as that of distributed cognition, activity theory, or semiotic engineering, are seen as too obscure and difficult to be useful for everyday HCI practitioners. It is to the credit of de Souza and her colleagues that over the years they have produced a body of work that is not only conceptual, but presents many worked-through examples of how this approach can have practical consequences for the design of systems. While it might seem that the take-up of some of the core ideas of this approach has been rather slow within the mainstream HCI community, like a slow-burning fire, I believe that the influence of this work will grow over the years and come to play an important role in how we conceive of computer systems in the future.

A Truly 'Human-Centred' Computing?

The ideas behind the semiotic approach require us to reformulate the very notion of the "HCI" field, as the label appears too lightweight. Recently, there has been some discussion about the emergence of a supposedly "new" field, that of "Human–centred" computing (HCC) (e.g. Bannon 2004; Sebe 2010; Hoffman et al. 2010). A brief perusal of the contents of these publications shows a variety of topics being covered, such as human-computer interaction, ubiquitous computing, adaptive systems, intelligent interfaces, interactive media and social informatics. For some, the term HCC is simply used as a kind of "umbrella" term, encompassing a range of distinct research themes such as interaction design and intelligent systems, human-computer interaction, etc. without any detailed overarching conceptual framework – other than a general interest in the development of complex human-machine systems that pay close attention to human and social factors. In this view, HCC can simply be described in terms of an enumeration of the various topics and sub-fields that make it up.

On the other hand, for others, the term "human-centred" in such terms as "human-centred design", "human-centred systems" and "human-centred computing", implies a more specific theoretical and, in some cases, ethical, commitment to the design and development of technologies that augment already existing skills and expertise of human workers. From this perspective, a "human-centred" approach puts emphasis on how it is human actors, designers and users, who make meaning out of the sign manipulation being done via computer systems. People, not computers, make meaning from signs. Thus, interestingly, de Souza argues that her approach necessarily requires an ethics of communication that goes beyond a general ethical commitment. As she succinctly notes: "Because they push the designers into representing self-images and thinking of their communicative intent and strategies, HCI theories of semiotic extraction can also stimulate the development of a new ethics in HCI design. Although the UCD tradition has clearly established an ethics commitment with the users' needs and aspirations, it has not contributed much to an ethics of communication since UCD theories only talk about relations and interactions between users and systems — not about users and systems designers." This opens up a variety of topics for further investigation, for example, the ways in which computer applications and interfaces can impose an alien, technical language on workers, thus dis-empowering them. As Andersen (2001) notes" *Interfaces should not only be interpretable, they should also be verbalizable: use the user's work language as a starting point for designing the system"*. Here we can see an interesting opening to another body of work that has also had an influence on the HCI field, namely participatory design. One of the tenets of the approach is that both designers and workers must learn about each other's work languages and practices in order to design usable and effective systems (cf. Simonsen and Robertson 2013). This also opens up a discussion on the perspective we take as HCI researchers towards our human 'users', which at times has been patronizing or even occasionally demeaning, viewing people who have difficulty with learning a new technical vocabulary as stupid. This latter viewpoint raises serious ethical and practical concerns, as I have noted elsewhere (Bannon 1986b, 2011).

Concluding Remarks

The field of HCI has grown considerably since the early 1980's – in terms of the size of the community, its diversity, and the amount of research conducted and published. However, to the scientific outsider, the conceptual underpinnings of the field are hard to discern and still open to question. After the early domination of the human information processing approach, there has been a brief flirtation with a variety of other frameworks such as activity theory, grounded theory, and situated action approaches, but much of the more recent HCI work has tended to eschew any discussions of theoretical import, focusing instead on more mundane practical matters. This is a shame, as without a coherent intellectual foundation, research becomes fragmented and poorly conceived. As Kurt Lewin (1951) once said: 'There is nothing so practical as a good theory'.

de Souza, in bringing a semiotic perspective and marrying it to an engineering approach, thus producing her Semiotic Engineering framework, has provided us with a richly nuanced conceptual framework within which to understand our research explorations. Her work links theory, method and practice in insightful and significant ways. It has been honed over many years, in collaboration with colleagues at her University, PUC-Rio, and elsewhere in Brazil, and has produced a large research corpus in its own right. Undoubtedly, as more people take the time to become familiar with this approach, it will grow in influence. In addition, she has devoted much time and effort in developing HCI education and training locally in Brazil and Latin America, as well as contributing on the world stage. It is a pleasure to acknowledge her significant contribution to the HCI field, and beyond, here in this Festschrift.

References

Andersen PB (1990) A theory of computer semiotics. Cambridge University Press, Cambridge
Andersen PB (2001) What semiotics can and cannot do for HCI. Knowl-Based Syst 14(8):419–424
Bannon L (1986a) Computer-mediated communication. In: Norman DA, Draper SW (eds) User centered system design: new perspectives on human-computer interaction. Lawrence Erlbaum Associates, Hillsdale
Bannon L (1986b) Issues in design: some notes. In: Norman DA, Draper SW (eds) User centered system design: New perspectives on human-computer interaction. Lawrence Erlbaum Associates, Hillsdale
Bannon L (2004) "Human-centred" computing: a new perspective? In: Andersen KV, Vendelo MT (eds) The past and future of information systems. Elsevier/Butterworth-Heinemann Information Systems Series, Amsterdam
Bannon L (2011) Reimagining HCI: toward a more human-centred perspective. ACM Interact 18(4):50–57
Bannon L, Bødker S (1991) Beyond the interface: encountering artifacts in use. In: Carroll JM (ed) Designing interaction: psychology at the human-computer interface. Cambridge University Press, New York, pp 227–253
Bannon L, Kaptelinin V (2000) From human-computer interaction to computer-mediated activity. In: Stephanidis C (ed) User interfaces for all – concepts, methods, and tools. Lawrence Erlbaum Associates, Mahwah, pp 183–202
Bødker S (1989) A human activity approach to user interfaces. Hum Comput Interact 4(3):171–195
de Souza CS (2012) Chapter 25: Semiotics and human-computer interaction. In: Soegaard M, Dam RF (eds) Encyclopedia of human-computer interaction, 2nd edn. Interaction Design Foundation, Aarhus
Hoffman RR, Bannon LJ, Sebe N (2010) Human-centered computing. In: Lansdale PA (ed) Encyclopedia of software engineering. CRC Press/Taylor & Francis, London
Lewin K (1951). Field theory in social science: selected theoretical papers, Cartwright D (ed). Harper & Row, New York
Nadin M (1988) Interface design and evaluation. In: Hartson R, Hix D (eds) Advances in human-computer interaction, vol 2. Ablex Publishing, Norwood, pp 45–100
Norman D (1986) Cognitive engineering. In: Norman DA, Draper SW (eds) User centered system design: new perspectives on human-computer interaction. Lawrence Erlbaum Associates, Hillsdale, pp 31–61
Sebe N (2010) Human-centered computing. In: Nakashima H, Aghajan H, Augusto J (eds) Handbook of ambient intelligence and smart environments. Springer, New York, pp 349–370. http://dx.doi.org/10.1007/978-0-387-93808-0_13
Simonsen J, Robertson T (eds) (2013) Routledge international handbook of participatory design. Routledge, New York
Winograd T, Flores F (1986) Understanding computers and cognition: a new foundation for design. Ablex, Norwood

Meaning and Ubiquitous Technologies

Susanne Bødker

Abstract This paper takes its starting-point in the current challenge of technologies everywhere, among us all the time. I recapitulate my research in computer-mediated activity to discuss mediation and meaning in the current wider context of multiplicity in terms of artifacts and activities. By discussing an example, I emphasize the somewhat ignored role of meaning in ubiquitous settings. This ignored role is a challenge to activity theoretical HCI as well as to semiotic engineering, I argue.

Introduction and Motivation

My starting point in this chapter is in computer-mediated human activity. It is increasingly clear that in order to analyze and design technological artifacts it is not sufficient to look at one artifact at a time, and one new artifact as substituting or replacing another. Human beings surround themselves with many artifacts, in many everyday activities, and what artifact is 'natural' for them to use is highly dependent on their individual past experiences, as well as of the shared practices of which they are part, and the technological possibilities offered to them, in (and outside) these communities of practice. In much of my recent work, I have been interested in understanding and conceptualizing multitudes of artifacts and the ways they are brought together in activities that people do together. However, this space seems populated with understandings of technologies that emphasize pick-up and use, or affordances/action possibilities, and my aim in this chapter is to also discuss *meaning*. In doing so I also open to some challenges that could potentially also be addressed, even better through computer semiotics.

S. Bødker (✉)
Aarhus University, Aarhus, Denmark
e-mail: bodker@cs.au.dk

S.D.J. Barbosa, K. Breitman (eds.), *Conversations Around Semiotic Engineering*, DOI 10.1007/978-3-319-56291-9_3

Multi-mediation and Meaning

In my work (with Peter Bøgh Andersen) on multi-mediation, we combined semiotics and activity theory (Bødker and Bøgh Andersen 2005) in order to address the duality of tool and sign, of acting and creating meaning, in a meditational triangle model. We largely share the semiotic background also described in de Souza (2005). The starting point was that, even though there are many work studies that account for instrumental, communicative, and cognitive aspects of work we found the need for a model that integrate these aspects. We found inspiration in the following quote from Vygotsky:

> The tool's function is to serve as the conductor of human influence on the object of activity; it is externally oriented; it must lead to changes in objects. It is a means by which human external activity is aimed at mastering and triumphing over, nature. The sign, on the other hand, changes nothing in the object of a psychological operation. It is a means of internal activity aimed at mastering oneself; the sign is internally oriented. (Vygotsky 1962, p. 55).

Inspired by Wells we analyzed co-occurring mediators, rather than one at a time:

> Thus, material and semiotic actions should not be thought of as mutually exclusive alternative forms of joint activity. Frequently, they occur simultaneously or alternate as phases in the same activity; in either case they are in important ways complementary. (Wells 2002, p. 50).

We proposed a model that includes juxtaposed mediators, and situations where language mediation is heavily intertwined with instrumental mediation, and hence mediation is not only about acting but also about creating meaning.

Following this, I have worked to address mediation in settings of multiple artifacts and discussed artifact ecologies and the ways technological artifacts are brought together. This may be in configurations that change over time, due to people's changing needs or as e.g. new technological solutions becoming available. Bødker and Klokmose (2012) note that:

> If we think of the artifact ecologies we surround ourselves with, they most often consist of multiple artifacts built for similar purposes but with slight variations and no clear delineation of when to use which artifact" (…) "Artifacts come and go; they can break and be replaced, or their function becomes obsolete due to changing circumstances, activities or because of newly acquired skills.

In addition, in this work, we proposed that users' shared capacities and experiences are not only based on individual acting and learning in the world, rather they are bound to shared practices, joint activities, etc., in artifact ecologies. So mastering one's activity is also about mastering oneself, in communication with one's community.

We have developed and used the Human-Artifact Model (Bødker and Klokmose 2011) as a means to analyze the use of artifacts in context of use and their artifact ecology. The analytical scheme of the Human-Artifact Model combines analyses of human experiences and artifacts, and addresses the tensions between human skills and capacity on the one hand, and the action possibilities and affordances offered by the artifact on the other. This is done on three levels reflecting the activity hierarchy: Activity, action, and operation. These levels provide three sets of analytical glasses, each of which focuses on an important aspect of human activity: Motivation (by asking why?), goal-orientation (by asking what?) and operation (by asking how?). In continuation of Christiansen (1996), activity is not only about human action through mediating artifacts, but also a process through which people create meaning in their practice while participating in a community of practice.

With Vygotsky I see human action as both internally and externally oriented, as directed towards others as well as towards things. Bødker and Klokmose (2016) point out how Bødker and Bøgh Andersen (2005) propose that the development of instrumental skills goes hand in hand with the formation of concepts. "*Humans are compulsive interpreters*", Bødker & Bøgh Andersen state, and point out that learning a new application should be seen not only as a development of skills but also as a process of concept formation and stabilization of language.

Design and Appropriation

With de Souza (2005) the connection from mediation and meaning to design and appropriation is rather evident, or as Christiansen (1996) discusses it, how are computer artifacts designed so that users care for them?

In Bødker and Christiansen (2012) we draw parallels to Bakhtin, who (acc. to Wertsch's (1998) p. 54) talks about language and how a word is first somebody else's and then, when being picked up, becomes half someone else's half one's own. It becomes one's own only when populated with one's own intentions, one's "accent", when one appropriates it. We point out that not all artifacts submit equally easily to appropriation, some stubbornly resist, and some remain alien. According to Wertsch (*ibid.*), appropriation requires action by the user (using the artifact), at the same time as the resistance is both socio-cultural and physical. We cannot make an artifact do whatever we want, individually or collectively. The environment, the community and its materials talk back.

Bødker and Klokmose (2016) look at the relationship between design and use in their discussion of conceptual blending. According to Fauconnier and Turner (2008), conceptual blending is the human ability to combine multiple conceptual spaces into one emergent one, called a blend, that shares and combines traits of the input spaces, while providing an emergent structure for reasoning and acting beyond the individual input spaces. According to Fauconnier & Turner (*ibid.*), the way we construct meaning is a highly dynamic process and constantly in development through blending, deblending, etc. The development of blends is not only individual, but happens on a cultural level as well. Bødker and Klokmose (2016) point out how designers' conceptual blends may differ significantly from users' blends, the latter difficult to presume and prescribe. This does not mean that the conceptual blends, which designers seed in and through the new design (also e.g. in manuals), do not matter to users. Rather, they can certainly be more or less useful seeds for the users' appropriation of the design. This is why it matters if the design can become the user's own, conceptually populated with their 'local' accents.

Conceptual blends are not one-to-one, and blends happen on multiple levels, as Bødker and Klokmose (2016) show. Multiplicity happens in many forms: The concepts get borrowed and appropriated from many domains, some of which are meaningful to the particular use activity, while others are either brought in as e.g. analogies, by the designers, or they are sheer historical reminiscences. The activity theoretical layering of activity, action and operations points out that blends may consist of concepts helping the user deal with why, while yet others point at what or how.

Local Area Artwork – An Example

Local Area Artwork (LAA) (Bødker and Polli 2014; Bødker et al. 2014; Bødker and Klokmose 2016) is a ubicomp system to explore location-specific collaborative text production in a local space. (Bødker 2015) (Figs. 1 and 2):

> We worked with a contemporary art venue, specifically one exhibition by a local art collective. In this, and in collaboration with artists and curator, conventional curatorial descriptions were replaced by collaboratively written texts on digital panels. The conventional curatorial descriptions of artworks, placed in the art gallery, were replaced by texts on digital panels collaboratively written and re-written by visitors during the exhibition, using

Fig. 1 Local Area Artwork in the art gallery

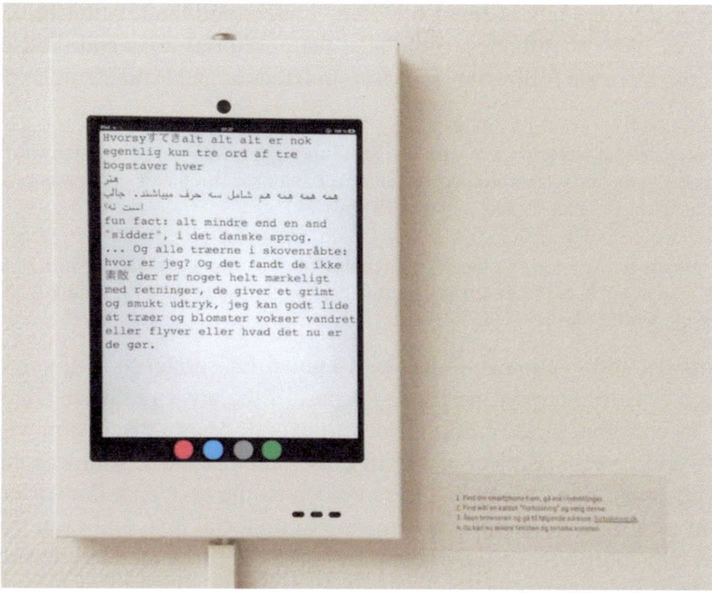

Fig. 2 The iPad panel with instruction for use

their personal mobile devices as mediators. The system detected when visitors were in close proximity of an artwork and redirected their browsers to the respective editable text. With LAA, a part of the usual curatorial activity of authoring interpretive descriptions for artworks was opened up for participation by anyone in the space—visitors, artists, curators, staff, etc. They could participate through their collaborative interpretation of artworks, or whatever they chose to add, and the format was basically that of a one-page co-produced text to be edited and reedited.

LAA was attempting to make the existing interpretative role of the audience explicit, visible and shared (Bødker 2015) by enabling co-interpretation among audience members in the physical space. This was done through a combination of hyper-local access to writing on the iPad panels placed next to the art pieces and an explicit choice of the designer to make these look very much like the well-known A4-sheet curatorial texts placed next to art in galleries. Access to writing and editing these texts was provided through smartphones brought to the gallery by the visitors themselves.

The use of phones had familiar yet surprising features that challenged the here-and-now togetherness of people in the exhibition space. People felt that instead of discussing art with those that they were with, they were focusing on their cellphone and a discussion with people who were not present, and whom they did not know. At the same time the phones were familiar and used in a new situation, interacting with something (the text, the art piece or the artist, perhaps, as discussed in Bødker and Polli 2014, Bødker et al. 2014) that was not clear to users. While the panels shifted the relationship between the art pieces, the curation, and the discussions of the audience, they were not perceived or appropriated in the gallery the way it had been imagined. Users talked about how they understood the relationships between the art pieces, the smartphones, the iPads, the curatorial texts and their company while visiting as in the following (see more in (Bødker and Polli 2014, Bødker et al. 2014)):

> when I saw the first work in there with an iPad, I thought it was just part of that work. So it was, I thought, the artist tries to make the audience interact. But then I saw it was at most of the works. Then I realized it was… I don't know (#6)

> I think, maybe to me it kind of means a lot that while you stand next to the work of art that you can read about it. So I think that the artist has [to choose to have it.] I think it has to be a part of the work of art (#10V).

Fundamentally, and in contrast to the well-known A4 curatorial text, users were in doubt about how to interpret the texts—as part of the artwork, hence coming from the artist, as curation, hence coming from an expert, or as a discussion with fellow visitors. In addition, in (Bødker and Polli 2014), the Facebook wall was introduced as a metaphor that illustrated how users perceived the text; as a flow of comments rather than as an open, yet coherent, piece of curatorial text, and even though the timeframe was short it seemed that the panels were appropriated by the audience as a discussion flow more than a piece of text.

LAA supports multiple actions and activities/purposes, in particular text can be produced (locally) and read (locally or on the website). The curatorial text can be handled by more users, mainly over time, through their own individual smartphones. However, as described, users found it confusing *whom* they were interacting with and about what. This shifted the focus from people who were together, to people who came after, or were absent, and because people found it confusing whether they were communicating with other spectators or with e.g. the artist. The role of the artist, the curator and others was unclear and invisible and in that manner the orientation around the common artifact was only for those co-present in the location, whereas other users were left more obscure, as can be seen in the quotes above.

Orientation towards other people around LAA is not only a matter of recognizing and reflecting on the here-and-now coming together of a group of users, but also a matter of how this unfolds over time, in changing and only partly visible configurations, which would seem to add new layers to both how we may understand appropriation, and how we design, and engage users in such design.

In the immediate appropriation of LAA, we see the role of the Facebook wall or a discussion thread as a more useful metaphor than that of a sheet of text. This has implications for the extent to which users are reluctant to edit the texts of other users, etc. Some expressed that they were participating in the artistic expression of the artworks, while others participated through a stream of commentaries.

The use of smartphones challenged the here-and-now togetherness of people in the exhibition space. The iPad panels seemed to shift involvement, engagement, commitment, and group action from happening among a group of visitors toward an engagement that is on the one hand for people individually (drawing attention away from the group), and on the other hand opening for involvement and commitment toward other groups—either other visitors over time or groups of artists, curators, and staff. As a matter of fact, the analyses of Bødker et al. (2014), Bødker and Polli (2014) and Bødker and Klokmose (2016) of the LAA point out that there is essentially a huge gap between what the LAA seems to have been designed for, and the meaning that users put into it: the Local Area Artwork example demonstrates how layers of blends are constituted across the levels of why, what, and how (Bødker and Klokmose 2016), but also that the blends intended by the designers are different from those developed by users, sometimes in rather unexpected ways.

Wrapping Up

LAA supports multiple actions and activities/purposes, in particular text can be produced (locally) and read (locally or on the website). With this example in mind we may ask: How may we find way of making clearer the shared meaning, in particular in such use where people come and go, where both professionals and non-professionals play a role, and where it is desirable for users to interact through well-known artifacts?

Orientation towards other people mediated by multiple artifacts is not only a matter of recognizing and reflecting on the here-and-now coming together of a group of users, as it is a matter of how this unfolds over time, in changing and only partly visible configurations, which would seem to add new layers to both how we may understand appropriation, and how we design, and engage users in such design. This is a challenge to activity-theoretical HCI, but it seems to semiotic engineering as well.

I cannot speak to the long-term appropriation and local needs really, even though a lot has been said (in Bødker et al. 2014, Bødker and Polli 2014 and Bødker and Klokmose 2016) regarding the immediate understanding of the LAA by visitors to the art gallery. It would seem, however, that it is not the local and idiosyncratic use that is at stake here as much as it is the general and across users understanding of what LAA is, across devices, users and situations. This seems to be an added challenge also to semiotic engineering, which seems so far to have focused mainly on meaning in the space between one designer and one user (or group of users) at the time.

Somehow, it seems that metaphors and conceptual blends could deserve some extra attention here, when it comes to shared meaning, across people and devices in these multiple and ubiquitous settings. This is because the main and last challenge in this is how designers may create ubiquitous technologies that do not just enter the artifact ecology and raise new action possibilities (which is what I think ubiquitous computing (ubicomp) has done so far), but also creates the semiotic foundation for supporting meaning-making, by people together, both in the longer and immediate perspectives.

Acknowledgements This work is based on my collaboration with many fellow researchers over many years. Thanks to all for putting up with me. Regarding this chapter, I would in particular acknowledge Ellen Christiansen and Clemens N. Klokmose for long-term collaboration and many interesting discussions over the years.

References

Bødker S (2015) Participation and sharing through technological artifacts – third wave HCI 10 years after, interactions. ACM, New York

Bødker S, Bøgh Andersen P (2005) Complex mediation. J Hum Comp Interac 20(4):353–402

Bødker S, Christiansen E (2012) Poetry in motion: appropriation of the world of apps. In: Proceedings of the 30th European Conference on Cognitive Ergonomics (ECCE'12). ACM, New York, pp 78–84

Bødker S, Polli AM (2014) Between initial familiarity and future use: a case of collocated collaborative writing. In: Proceedings of COOP 2014, Springer, pp 137–154

Bødker S, Klokmose CN (2011) The human-artifact model–an activity theoretical approach to artifact ecologies. Hum Comp Interac 26(4):315–371

Bødker S, Klokmose CN (2012) Dynamics in artifact ecologies. In: Proceedings of the 7th nordic conference on human-computer interaction: making sense through design, ACM, pp 448–457

Bødker S, Klokmose CN (2016) Dynamics, multiplicity and conceptual blends in HCI. In: Proceedings of the 2016 CHI Conference on Human Factors in Computing Systems (CHI'16). ACM, New York, pp 2538–2548

Bødker S, Klokmose CN, Korn M, Polli AM (2014) Participatory IT in semi- public spaces. In: Proceedings of the 8th Nordic Conference on Human- Computer Interaction: Fun, Fast, Foundational (NordiCHI'14). ACM, pp 765–774

Christiansen E (1996) Tamed by a rose: computers as tools in human activity. In: Nardi, B. Context and Consciousness: Activity Theory and Human Computer Interaction, pp 175–198

de Souza CS (2005) The semiotic engineering of human-computer interaction. MIT Press, Cambridge, MA

Fauconnier G, Turner M (2008) The way we think: conceptual blending and the mind's hidden complexities. Basic Books, New York

Vygotsky LS (1962) Thought and language. MIT Press, Cambridge, MA

Wells G (2002) The role of dialogue in activity theory. Mind Cult Act 9(1):43–66

Wertsch J (1998) Mind as action. Oxford University Press, New York

Exploring Richer Ecologies Between Designers and Users

Gerhard Fischer

Abstract The fundamental contribution of Semiotic Engineering to human-computer interaction (HCI) has been to propose and establish a discourse to conceptualize HCI not primarily about how users interact with computers but as computer-mediated communication between designers and users at interaction time. It represents an important contribution to explore the future of HCI beyond the focus of usability and interfaces. In our own research over the last few decades, we have also explored alternative approaches to create richer frameworks and ecologies on how designers and users can interact in the design of computational artifacts. This contribution briefly describes some of these approaches by characterizing the problems that they addressed and the potential solutions that they explored.

Introduction

Semiotic Engineering views HCI as "computer-mediated communication between designers and users at interaction time. The system speaks for its designers in various types of conversations specified at design time. These conversations communicate the designers' understanding of who the users are, what they know the users want or need to do, in which preferred ways, and why. The designers' message to users includes even the interactive language in which users will have to communicate back with the system in order to achieve their specific goals." (De Souza and Leitao 2009, p. vi). Reconceptualizing HCI not primarily as interactions between users and systems, but as communication processes between designers and users with the computational environments serving as media, emphasizes different design challenges, frameworks, and objectives.

Some of Clarisse Sieckenius de Souza's research and our research explored some closely related issues, e.g. to conceptualize software development (De Souza et al. 2016; Fischer and Nakakoji 1992) as reflective practice (Schön 1983), we have also explored alternative approaches to Semiotic Engineering to create richer frameworks and ecologies on how designers and users can interact in the design of

G. Fischer (✉)
University of Colorado at Boulder, Boulder, CO 80309, USA
e-mail: gerhard@colorado.edu

S.D.J. Barbosa, K. Breitman (eds.), *Conversations Around Semiotic Engineering*, DOI 10.1007/978-3-319-56291-9_4

computational artifacts. While some of these research activities (addressing problems, creating frameworks, and designing, developing, and assessing systems) have taken place some time ago, this brief contribution tries to argue that at least some aspects still represent challenges today complementing and enriching Semiotic Engineering approaches in exploring the future of HCI beyond usability and interfaces (Greenberg and Buxton 2008).

Advances and Reconceptualizations of HCI

A considerable amount of research has been conducted in HCI during the last 30 years. The early research efforts centered on complementing professionally dominated design with user-centered design (Norman and Draper 1986) and they were driven by *technological* developments that line-oriented interfaces were replaced by WIMP interfaces and by *societal* developments that computer users were coming from all fields rather than being only computer scientists. An important vision (at the time) was provided by Newell and Card (1985) in the mid-eighties to conceptualize HCI at different time scales (see Fig. 1).

As the envisioned developments started to take place in reality, namely the time scales becoming longer (i.e.: weeks, months, and years rather than seconds or minutes), the research challenges were grounded in a world in which social theory became increasingly relevant and complemented the research activities focused on

	Time	Action	Memory	Theory
(sec)	(common units)			
10^9	(decades)	Technology	Culture	Social and Organizational
10^8	(years)	System	Development	
10^7	(months)	Design	Education	
10^6	(weeks)	Task	Education	
10^5	(days)	Task	Skill	Bounded Rationality
10^4	(hours)	Task	Skill	
10^3	(ten mins)	Task	LTM	
10^2	(minutes)	Task	LTM	
10	(ten secs)	Unit task	LTM	Psychological
1	(secs)	Operator	STM	
10^{-1}	(tenths)	Cycle time	Buffers	
10^{-2}	(centisecs)	Signal	Integration	Neural And Biochemical
10^{-3}	(millisecs)	Pulse	Summation	

Fig. 1 Time scales of human action (Newell and Card 1985, p. 226)

Table 1 Overview of themes

Theme	Problem	Potential solution explored
"usable *versus* useful" to "usable *and* useful"	Reality is not user-friendly requiring high-functionality environments	Learning on demand, achieve external simplicity with internal complexity
Bridging situation and system models	People (e.g.: designers and users) live in different conceptual environments	Building a variety of different bridges to creates common ground and shared understadning
Human problem-domain interaction	Thin spread of application knowledge	Domain-oriented design environments
Meta-design	Closed systems cannot models open and changing worlds	Empowering users to act as designers; breaking down the strict separation between designers and users; democratizing innovation

the isolated actor. These developments required that HCI research got more closely linked with theories and developments from education, development, and cultural change.

Our own research methodology was grounded in the philosophical approach of Popper focused on *"the search for knowledge does not start from perceptions, or observations, or collection of data or facts, but it starts from problems."* (Popper 1959). Table 1 provides an overview of the topics of our research that were driven by addressing problems that HCI research needed and needs to address.

From "Usable *versus* Useful" to "Usable *and* Useful"

HCI approaches have traditionally focused on making systems more *usable*—often by reducing the expressive power of the systems and their interfaces. This approach has focused on designing systems for casual users who are assumed to be using the system for the first time, for only few times, and for simple activities. Walk-up-and-use systems, such as ATMs (Automated Teller Machines), are examples of low-threshold, low-ceiling systems; they are be easy to understand and use without prior experience, but are limited in the power they afford users.

In contrast, systems for professional use need to be *useful*; these systems are used daily for a wide range of activities within their application domains, such as information gathering, representing design situations, exploring alternative and sharing work with colleagues. The needs of professionals have traditionally been addressed with high-threshold and high-ceiling systems that can be difficult to use at first, but over time are learned and support users to perform a wide range of tasks.

Designing useful *and* usable high-functionality environments (HFEs) (Fischer 1993) requires that we go beyond the traditional HCI notions of "usability" and "ease of use," to design and assess HFEs that interact with designers, individually and collaboratively, as they struggle with large and ill-defined problems over long periods of time.

HFEs are a result that "reality is not user friendly"—therefore many tools are required (Buxton 2002). Users can be overwhelmed by having to decide which way is best, rather than merely finding a single way to do the task. In many cases, HFEs:

- create a *"tool-mastery burden"* requiring users to spend considerable effort to master the system before they can do anything useful with it thereby outweighing the advantage of the broad functionality offered;
- most of their functionality goes unused, and users need support to find the tools or information they need when they need it; and
- no system, regardless of its size and complexity can achieve complete coverage of large and changing domains. Inevitably, some information will become obsolete, and breakdowns due to missing knowledge will occur.

To make systems useful *and* usable HFEs needed to be improved in their ability to interact with users by giving them "knowledge" about the problem domain, about communication processes, and about the users who interacted with the system. Our approaches to achieve these objectives have been:

- to address the "tool-mastery burden" with domain-oriented systems that allow users to communicate with the problem domain rather than the computer. Human problem-domain interaction allows users to spend more of their time thinking about their tasks, and less time worrying about communicating with the computer;
- to address the "unknown functionality" challenge by developing techniques to give systems the ability to determine what information and functionality might be relevant to the tasks a user is trying to accomplish, and to actively present users with this information without having them to explicitly ask for it; and
- to address the "impossibility of complete coverage" challenge by viewing systems as open-ended and continuously adapted by the people who use them in their day-to-day work.

Bridging Situation and System Models

The interaction between users and systems is a conversation in a vocabulary and language determined by the input the system is able to accept and process. In many systems, information is structured around a description of the system, not around an analysis of the problems users address when using the system.

Compared to humans, computers are able to respond to a very limited range of input (Suchman 1987). To get something done on a computer system, users must provide input to the system that is within the limited range to which the computer is programmed to respond. To talk about the discrepancies between the way a human thinks of a problem and the limited inputs to which the system is capable of responding, we have used the terms *situation* and *system model* (Kintsch 1998):

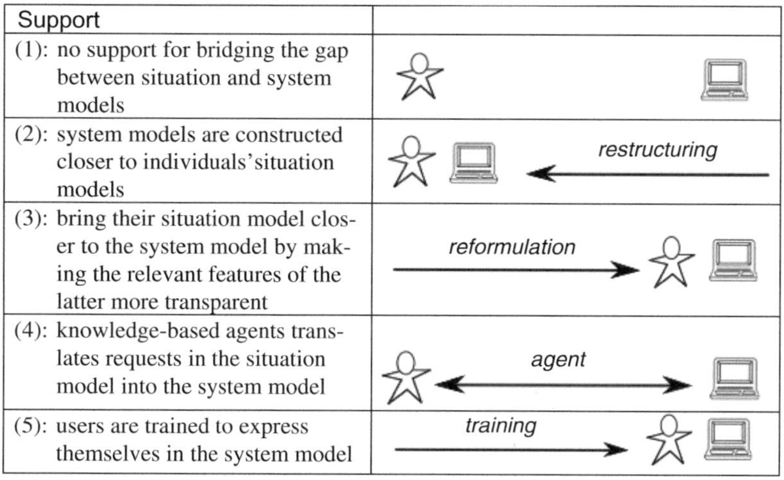

Fig. 2 Different relationships between situation and system models

- the *situation model* is a mental representation of the situation as the user sees it, including the problems motivating a task, general ideas for finding a solution, and a characterization of the desired goal state;
- the *system model* consists of a set of operations that, when invoked, will result in the desired solution. These operations must all be within the repertory of the system: for each operation there must exist one or more commands, depending upon context, to execute it.

At the level of the situation model, goals refer to actions and states in the users' problem space and are articulated in terms of what they want. Goals may be precise or imprecise, but the important point is that they are structured or named according to the system model (Furnas et al. 1987) rather than in terms of the application problem to be solved (Curtis et al. 1988). Figure 2 illustrates several different approaches to dealing with the gap between situation and system models:

- In (1), there is no support for bridging this gap. In this case, people frequently have difficulties in solving problems or finding information, because they are unable to communicate within the scope of the system model, even if they have a clear understanding of what they want to do.
- In (2), a new system model is constructed which is closer to an individual's situation model and hence more intuitive and easier to use representing the objective of human problem-domain interaction.
- In (3), users are supported to bring their situation model closer to the system model by making the relevant features of the latter more transparent. An example of this approach is the paradigm of retrieval by reformulation (Williams 1984). This theory postulates that people naturally think about categories of things not in terms of formal attributes but in terms of examples. Through presenting examples of objects retrieved by queries, the system reveals its system model and

helps the user to incrementally formalize their query to better match the system model.

- In (4), a knowledge-based agent translates a request in the situation model into the system model requiring the agent to have enough knowledge to assist users in mapping tasks conceptualized in their situation model to the system model.
- In (5), users are trained to express themselves in the system model. This is the case with many skilled expert users, who have gained over time a familiarity with the system model such that their situation model matches the system model.

Human Problem-Domain Interaction

If the most important role for computation is to provide people with a powerful medium for expression, then the medium should support them in working on the task, rather than require them to focus their intellectual resources on the medium itself. When users suffer from a tool mastery burden, their tasks fade to the background while effort is put toward mastering the tool. To bring tasks to the forefront, computers must become "*invisible*" (Norman 1991) allowing users to put the majority of their efforts toward interacting with the problem domain, rather than the computer.

The shift from "human computer interaction" to "human problem-domain interaction" (Fischer and Lemke 1988) puts users, being the owners of problems, in charge freeing them from a reliance on computer specialists. In analogy to eliminating the power of scribes in the middle ages (when most people were unable to read and write), a major goal of HCI should be "to take the control of computational media out of the hands of high-tech scribes."

Professional programmers and end-users define the endpoints of a continuum of computer users. The former like computers because they can program, and the latter because they get their work done. Techniques and languages enabling users to acquire computer literacy have been explored with *end-user development* (Lieberman et al. 2006; Nardi 1993). One objective of *end-user development* is to offer task-specific languages that take advantage of existing user knowledge (e.g., mathematicians already know the mathematical knowledge embedded in Mathematica, and accountants already know the conceptual model behind spreadsheets (Fischer and Rathke 1988)).

Meta-Design: Empowering Users to Act as Designers

Meta-design (Fischer and Giaccardi 2006) represents a theoretical framework, supported by innovative information and communication technologies, in which humans of all ages can participate as co-designers and pursue topics of interest, reformulate knowledge, express themselves creatively and appropriately, and produce and generate information rather than simply comprehend existing information.

In a world that is not predictable, improvisation, evolution, and innovation are more than luxuries—they are *necessities*. The challenge of design is not a matter of getting rid of the emergent, but rather of including it and making it an opportunity for more creative and more adequate solutions to problems. Many design approaches force all the design intelligence to the earliest part of the design process, when everyone knows the least about what is really needed.

Meta-design provides the foundations for *cultures of participation* (Fischer 2011) in which all users can act as active contributors at use time. In cultures of participation, users are allowed and empowered to make significant modifications when the need arises because, despite the best efforts at design time, systems need to be evolvable to fit new needs and account for changing tasks. Meta-design complements and transcends *participatory design* (Binder et al. 2011) that seeks to involve users more deeply in the process as co-designers by empowering them to propose and generate design alternatives themselves. Participatory design requires the social inclusion and active participation of the users at *design time* by bringing developers and users together to envision the contexts of use. Meta-design provided a foundation and it was further developed in long-term research project "The Envisionment and Discovery Collaboratory" (Arias et al. 2016), a table-top computing environment in which all stakeholders could participate as active contributors in personally meaningful problems.

Broad Impact

This contribution contrasts semiotic engineering with some alternative conceptual developments that we have pursued in our own research activities. There are numerous other frameworks developed that are relevant for the future of HCI. Three representative developments that I consider personally important to take into account will be briefly mentioned here: creativity support tools, social production, and libertarian paternalism.

Creativity support tools (Shneiderman 2007) enable new forms of expression for individuals, groups and communities. Their focus is to move HCI beyond usability, usefulness, and productivity objectives to support creativity, innovation, and to form new alliances between research communities in the creative practices and information, and in communication technologies.

Social production (Benkler 2006) provides the foundation that social media enables many more individuals to communicate their observations and their viewpoints to many others, thereby changing control and fostering new levels creativity in digital cultures. Social production emphasizes that technology alone does not determine social structure: it creates feasibility spaces for new social and cultural practice. Meta-design supports social production by facilitating and supporting the creation of consumer-generated content and it enriches individual autonomy substantively by creating an environment built less around control and more around facilitating action.

Libertarian Paternalism (Thaler and Sunstein 2009) represents a fundamental concept applicable in many domains that it is both possible and legitimate for private and public institutions to affect behavior while also respecting freedom of choice of individuals belonging to these institutions. It argues that designers should consider themselves as choice architects thereby promoting a design methodology. The framework demonstrates that designer-imposed structures affecting users' choices are inevitable, and hence that a form of paternalism cannot be avoided but that the libertarian part allows users to override the choices made by designers.

Conclusions

Semiotic engineering has provided insights and theoretical foundations for HCI in the past and will continue to do so in the future. Beyond its impact on HCI, it has influenced many scientific fields including computer-mediated communication, multimedia-hypermedia systems, end user development, intelligent user interfaces, artificial intelligence, and various branches of software engineering. My hope is that the ideas and developments briefly discussed in this contribution can form an alliance with semiotic engineering to create elements for innovative frameworks in HCI that will make a difference with respect to the problems that we frame and solve, the questions that we ask, and the research activities that we undertake.

References

Arias EG, Eden H, Fischer G (2016) The Envisionment and Discovery Collaboratory (EDC): explorations in human-centered informatics. Morgan & Claypool Publishers, San Rafael

Benkler Y (2006) The wealth of networks: how social production transforms markets and freedom. Yale University Press, New Haven

Binder T, DeMichelis G, Ehn P, Jacucci G, Linde P, Wagner I (2011) Design things. MIT Press, Cambridge, MA

Buxton W (2002) Less is more (more or less). In: Denning PJ (ed) The invisible future – the seamless integration of technology in everyday life. McGraw-Hill, New York, pp 145–179

Curtis B, Krasner H, Iscoe N (1988) A field study of the software design process for large systems. Commun ACM 31(11):1268–1287

De Souza CS, Cerqueira RF d G, Afonso LM, Brandão RR d M, Ferreira JSJ (2016) Software developers as users: semiotic investigations in human-centered software development. Springer, New York

De Souza CS, Leitao CF (2009) Semiotic enginnering methods for scientific research in HCI. Morgan & Claypool Publishers, San Rafael

Fischer G (1993) Beyond human computer interaction: designing useful and usable computational environments. In: People and computers VIII: proceedings of the HCI'93 conference (Loughborough, England). Cambridge University Press, Cambridge, UK, pp 17–31
Fischer G (2011) Understanding, fostering, and supporting cultures of participation, ACM Interac XVIII. 3 (May + June 2011), pp 42–53
Fischer G, Giaccardi E (2006) Meta-design: a framework for the future of end user development. In: Lieberman H, Paternò F, Wulf V (eds) End user development. Kluwer Academic Publishers, Dordrecht, pp 427–457
Fischer G, Lemke AC (1988) Construction kits and design environments: steps toward human problem-domain communication. Human Comp Interac 3(3):179–222
Fischer G, Rathke C (1988) Knowledge-Based spreadsheet systems. In: Proceedings of AAAI-88, seventh national conference on artificial intelligence (St. Paul Mn), Morgan Kaufmann Publishers, San Mateo, pp 802–807
Fischer G, Nakakoji K (1992) Beyond the macho approach of artificial intelligence: empower human designers – do not replace them. Knowledge Based Syst J, Special Issue on AI in Design 5(1):15–30
Furnas GW, Landauer TK, Gomez LM, Dumais ST (1987) Vocabulary problem in human-system communication. Commun ACM 30(11):964–971
Greenberg S, Buxton B (2008) Usability evaluation considered harmful (some of the time). In: CHI 2008 proceedings. ACM, Florence, pp 111–120
Kintsch W (1998) Comprehension: a paradigm for cognition. Cambridge University Press, Cambridge, UK
Lieberman H, Paterno F, Wulf V (eds) (2006) End user development. Kluwer Publishers, Dordrecht
Nardi BA (1993) A small matter of programming. The MIT Press, Cambridge, MA
Newell A, Card SK (1985) The prospects for psychological science in human-computer interaction. Human-Computer Interaction 1(3):209–242
Norman D (1991) Cognitive artifacts. In: Carroll JM (ed) Designing interaction. Cambridge University Press, Cambridge, pp 17–38
Norman DA, Draper SW (eds) (1986) User-centered system design, new perspectives on human-computer interaction. Lawrence Erlbaum Associates Inc, Hillsdale
Popper KR (1959) The logic of scientific discovery. Basic Books, New York
Schön DA (1983) The reflective practitioner: how professionals think in action. Basic Books, New York
Shneiderman B (2007) Creativity support tools: accelerating discovery and innovation. Commun ACM 50(12):20–32
Suchman LA (1987) Plans and situated actions. Cambridge University Press, Cambridge, UK
Thaler RH, Sunstein CR (2009) Nudge—improving decisions about health, wealth, an happiness. Penguin Books, London
Williams MD (1984) What makes rabbit run? Int J Man Machine Stud *21*:333–352

6,000 Years of Programming Language Design: A Meditation on Eco's Perfect Language

Alan F. Blackwell

Abstract Fact 1: A programming language is a way of saying what should happen. Fact 2: Most programming languages can only be understood by experts. This short chapter discusses the implications of those two facts, in the light of many other languages that have historically been used by experts to specify what should happen. The semiotic argument underlying the discussion offers some parallels to Umberto Eco's classic "The Search for the Perfect Language".

Prologue

The true nature of the "computer" is not that it *computes*, but that it *communicates* – or rather, it is *people* who communicate, using computers. This truth was apparently creeping up on us for many years, and Clarisse Sieckenius de Souza was a pioneer among computer scientists in recognising the implications. Computers are machines for language. Semiotics (and especially Prof. de Souza's Semiotic Engineering (2005)) provides an invaluable guide to understanding what that means in practice. This chapter offers an unconventional diachronic perspective on one of the most transparently communicative aspects of computer science: the programming "language". De Souza and her colleagues have made valuable contributions to end-user programming – the branch of programming language design concerned with democratic access and broad empowerment (de Souza et al. 2016). Here, we consider how well those concerns have been accommodated in other languages.

6000 Years Ago

According to the Irish bishop James Ussher, God created the world with an act of language at around 6 pm on 22 October 4004 BC. This is surely the most powerful declarative programming language ever. But what was the operational

A.F. Blackwell (✉)
Computer Laboratory, University of Cambridge, Cambridge CB3 0FD, UK
e-mail: afb21@cam.ac.uk

S.D.J. Barbosa, K. Breitman (eds.), *Conversations Around Semiotic Engineering*, DOI 10.1007/978-3-319-56291-9_5

vocabulary – or keywords – of this language? God did not speak the words *let there be light* (God did not yet speak the Queen's English), or even the more Biblical Latin *fiat lux*, or Old Testament Hebrew אוֹר יְהִי. We do not know, because according to the scriptural story of the Tower of Babel, the original language of the Garden of Eden has been lost, and we are afflicted with variety in human language as a punishment, causing discord between people who speak different languages. Umberto Eco, in his popular book *The Search for the Perfect Language* (1995), describes the ways in which medieval scholars attempted to rediscover that original perfect language: the language in which God created the cosmos, and also conversed with Adam.

Stories and Mechanisms

This chapter offers a short reflection on programming language design, from the perspective of religious and scientific history. The relationship between 'academics' (of various kinds - philosophers, scientists and priests) and everyday people has been established in large part by the languages they use. I argue here that much programming language design replays the dynamics of those past generations.

There are certainly programming language designers who have assumed a somewhat prophetic aspect in their pronouncements, most famously Dijkstra's commandment that the GOTO is evil. But really we spend a lot more time trying to discover the fundamentals – for computer science researchers who come to programming language design as a mathematical exercise, it seems that there must be an original language of algorithms, discovered not invented, and that the huge variety of different languages that we see in practice represent a source of Babel-like confusion departing from the ideal.

Because mathematical languages are based on universally "true" (consistent and replicable) relations, mathematics has been useful since prehistoric times for specifying the world – whether a grand Egyptian pyramid or a humble farmer's field. But perhaps more fundamental than representing correspondences of physical quantities via numerical measurement and calculation, are languages for the discrete specification of thought and action: algorithmic sequence, iteration and selection.

The oldest of these discrete specification languages must surely be the language of weaving and other textiles, in which an artifact is narrated into existence, by a weaver who "tells a story" of threads passing in and out, over and under, forward and back. The narratives by which textiles become mathematical are especially explicit in the Andean quipu, which provides a tangible medium for computation and data storage.

In the same way that a quipu string offers a mechanically specified narrative, so the mechanician Joseph Marie Jacquard adapted the mechanical stories of eighteenth century clockwork automata to string together instructions for weaving. Over the next 100 years, the mechanical language of the punched card pile was adapted to Charles Babbage's Analytical Engine and Herman Hollerith's American census cards, demonstrating the power of tangible sequence for expressing and generating organized narratives of action in the world.

Weaving stories is ancient and universal, but also time-consuming – not to mention noisy and bulky when translated to cardboard and clockwork. If it were not for the practical necessity of tangible materials and machinery, these languages could have been far more elegant. The tension between elegance and convenience appears to be perennial. In programming language design, we have often seen near-religious debates about the use of languages that appear too convenient to be rigorous, as when Dijkstra complained that BASIC was rotting the minds of young programmers, or the current debate between block syntax languages and more respectable string parsing.

Are we still in search of the perfect programming language, like the medieval scholars described by Umberto Eco? Presumably such a language would reflect eternal and undeniable mathematical truths, rather than fallible human stories, actions, habits and beliefs? Of course, formal mathematics can coexist with less rational belief, so long as it restricts itself to describing regularities in the observed world rather than belief systems. For example, Greek philosophers and mathematicians of the classical period developed systematic uses of language that were independent of the rituals and belief systems of their era. As a result, these elite scholars could carry out their analytic work while maintaining (occasionally ironic) detachment from the language of popular religion and mythical stories.

Standardisation and Liberation

The standardised administrative literacy of the Roman empire created an environment in which the language of philosophers was merged with popular religion, building on the New Testament Christianity of St Paul and the gospel writers. Under the Romans, Latin became the standardised language of their empire – just like the programming language C, Latin "ran everywhere", meaning that instructions written in Latin could be used to specify actions in many different local contexts.

However, an interesting thing happened as standardised Latin became more widely applied and also more sophisticated. Although the Christian religion had originally been a religion of liberation (from Hebrew legal constraints and Roman economic ones), Latinate Christianity became the religion of empire. As with so many popular religions, an anti-elite movement turned into a new elite, embraced by rulers who created an infrastructure of cathedrals and monasteries under the direction of Rome.

Under the Roman empire, Latin had become a language of trade and law, and under the Roman papacy, it also became the professional language of religious ceremony and philosophical debate. The grammar and the lexicon became conventionalized through diligent scholarship, and young scholar-monks who learned Latin would gain a job for life. Like implementations of the lambda calculus, Latin became an artificial language - well defined, and a good basis for analysis, specification and control.

The problem with all this specialist scholarly material, and indeed the Bible itself, being written in Latin, was that ordinary people who did not understand Latin could not use this standardized language for their everyday analysis and specification tasks. Instead, ordinary people used languages they could understand, meaning that as the centuries passed, Europeans inherited two parallel language systems: one that was formally specified, standardized, and useful for theoretical work, and one vernacular language that people actually used.

This disconnection between formal religious language and vernacular end-user language was theologically problematic, precisely because the Bible offered a populist democratic message, in which individual believers were supposed to be freed from the formal apparatus of pharisaic ritual and state control. A new generation of populists including Wycliffe, Gutenberg and Luther realised that important things ought to be expressed in end-user language. The media technology of the printing press demanded a vernacular language that could be understood by readers outside the monasteries.

Is there any place for a specialist, and formally specified, language in an age of vernacular media? Although there are still people who read and write Latin, the only place it is still used for business and philosophy is in the Vatican. This is not where we want our programming languages to be in 500 years time.

The Modern Monastery: From Latin to Mathematics

Of course, programming languages are also scientific tools, not purely for everyday description of actions and policies. Perhaps the highest achievement of English renaissance science, Isaac Newton's *Philosophiæ Naturalis Principia Mathematica*, (mathematical principles of natural philosophy) following the traditions of monastic scholarship, was published not only in Latin, but in the language of mathematics. This book became the archetype of elite scholarship in my own university at Cambridge.

Newton continued the tradition of the classical philosophers and of his contemporary astronomers by applying these languages to description of the observed world (rather than human experience or beliefs) – the enterprise of "natural philosophy". While anybody might observe a planet or a rainbow, it is translation of these observations into formal language that provides the basis for science. So just as with the separation between vernacular religion and Latin theology, natural philosophy introduced specialist ways of describing everyday experience that excluded the 'end-users' of uneducated society.

An interesting consequence of these developments, within the rigid English class system, was that the language of mathematics, just like Latin before it, became a signifier of educational achievement among the scholarly elite. Since Newton, Cambridge students have been subjected to a competitive examination of mathematical skill – the 'Mathematical Tripos'. Those who demonstrate first class skills are the 'Wranglers', with the best awarded the title of 'Senior Wrangler', and themselves destined for a life of recognition for supreme academic ability (Warwick 2003).

From the time of Newton until the present, the 'programming language' of mathematical argument and demonstration has served as the measure of academic excellence, over and above its clear utility. This was still pretty much the case when my own department was formed as the 'Mathematical Laboratory' in 1937. Charles Babbage had been one of the successors to Newton as Lucasian professor of mathematics, and in an alternative history, Turing could also have been. The Mathematical Laboratory did maths, in an era when programming languages were mathematical languages, such as FORTRAN the Formula Translator.

Although scholars in the tradition of Babbage and Turing apply formal languages to practical problems, many universities retain an admiration for skill in symbol manipulation rather than practical application. One of my colleagues reported a conference discussion recapitulating Dijkstra's rejection of BASIC, but this time contrasting the Python language (designed for accessibility) with the ML language (designed for mathematical elegance): *John Ousterhout asked whether it would be unfair to characterise ML as a language for people with excess IQ points. Someone in the audience volunteered that ML is a standard undergraduate programming language at Cambridge, without saying whether that meant "yes" or "no."* (Jeff Haemer, quoted in Stajano 2000)

In this modern monastery, we see uses of mathematical language that echo those of scholastic Latin. Like Latin, formal mathematics draws away from being a standardised and utilitarian way of describing the world. As these languages became more precise, and more precisely defined, they also became less approachable – a game for specialists rather than a tool for end-users.

The Vulgar Vernaculars: Natural Science and Engineering

The problem is that the everyday world seems to defy our ability to analyse and specify it in well-defined ways. Artificial languages with agreed rules and quantification are useful for some purposes, for example when we need to objectively compare the performance scores of the Senior Wrangler to those of other mathematicians lower down in the elite ranking. Well defined languages work fine in monasteries and universities, where everyone agrees to play the same game by the same rules, but others complain when monks and professors insist that the rest of the world use their rules - especially when those rules mean that the monks and professors win the game!

There was a revolt, of a kind, when advocates of scientific enquiry argued that one should not simply sit exams, but observe the world, collect evidence, and analyse it in order to understand the nature of Creation. This was a spirit that led to the geology of Adam Sedgwick (making our story a little longer than 6000 years), and of course to Charles Darwin. Natural Philosophy, Natural History, and Natural Science campaigned for new kinds of university work that collected specimens and conducted experiments. When combined with new mathematics, physics was transformed.

Through the nineteenth century, formal languages of description and analysis interacted with the sources of economic wealth – the industrial revolution and the steam engine – to ensure that physics was the most prestigious of all the Natural Sciences. In the heyday of the steam engine and mechanical engineering, the language of physics had become the "programming language" for the technology of the day. The foundations of electrical engineering can be found in the systematic mathematical descriptions of experimental apparatus. Experimentalists and industrialists talked the same language, with some simply a little more entrepreneurial than others – much the same as today!

This introduces a problem for academic study, though – Natural Science was democratic, because anybody can go and observe. If we study things that we make ourselves, then there is the danger of once again producing a language of academic irrelevance, rather than practical value. This does not seem to have happened to the specification language of physics and mechanism (although relentless campaigning is needed to keep the STEM curriculum in schools), but is there a danger that it might happen to the specification languages of computing?

Herb Simon argued that we cannot regard computer science as a natural science, in which we go out and observe the world. It is instead a science of the artificial – studying things that we are also making. Experimental sciences aim to control and understand *existing* phenomena around us. Sciences of the artificial aim to create *new* phenomena. Computer programming is one of the areas in human life where we make new things, and study what we make – the things we make and study in computer science are artefacts of language, just as much as music, novels or writing poetry are.

These are not analogies that are welcome to the computer scientist, because they suggest that we might need to study people, rather than natural phenomena. Of course it is possible to study people, but rather annoyingly, they don't stand still while we do it. When Newton observes light in a prism, the observations that he makes will be the same when he looks again. The prism does not change its mind, to split colours in a different order. However, when we observe and describe a person's behaviour, that person can (and often does) then decide to behave completely differently.

A Science of Programming Languages?

People are annoying and inconsistent. Making programming languages would be so much easier, if only people weren't involved! One way to avoid this annoyance is to make programming languages that are designed specifically for philosophical investigation – like medieval scholastic Latin, or the exercises of the Mathematical

Tripos. However, a persistent irritation for the programming language research community is that the programming language is a user interface, between the programmer (who is a fallible person) and the computer.

The tension between the desire for mathematical precision, and the annoying variability of end-users, underlies many debates that I see in the programming languages community. People who have been trained as mathematicians and physicists are incredibly disappointed, when they are told that the well-defined languages and predictable experiments they are used to might not work so well if the programming language is actually going to be used by people. There are suggestions that we need a "physics" of language (Moody 2009), that will simply tell us by mechanical analysis what the best design choices would be. Or there are calls for "evidence-based" programming language design (Kaijanaho 2015), in which randomised controlled trials are used to compare alternative language designs for usability, in the manner of a pharmaceutical trial.

The unfortunate truth is that these approaches are only partially effective, when it comes to the sciences of the artificial. Computer Science perennially faces the old joke that if an academic discipline has the word "science" in its name, this is a sign that it is not a science. If we accept Herb Simon's definition, then we are science of the artificial, studying the things we build. We can also use classical experimental techniques, so long as we are carrying out classical experiments – speeding up a compiler or reducing the number of iterations in a type-checking algorithm.

But things get difficult when people are involved – and programming languages involve people. Perhaps this is not even a science of the artificial - because we don't make people, and we can't tell them what to do. Instead, we have to observe and understand them – even when they are annoying and inconsistent, which is not often fun. However, there is an approach to studying annoying and inconsistent people in a scientific way, which seems useful for studying programming. It's also useful for studying other artificial phenomena that involve people, such as music, poetry or religion. Furthermore, it helps us understand some of the dynamics I have been describing, in which perfectly sensible philosophical systems, academic skills and artificial languages turn out to struggle when faced with popular everyday and political problems.

The twentieth century philosopher Husserl, aware of all these problems, suggested that the *natural* sciences of the nineteenth century had to be supplemented with a science of *culture*. It was necessary to develop rigorous methods of observation and analysis that could be used to understand how people create and consume culture. I would argue that programming is a part of modern culture, far more than it is a part of science, and that the programming language is as much a human language (or at least a user interface) as it is a mathematical notation.

Software has become a cultural medium, in which people want to have fun, communicate, be entertained and so on. Scientific understanding of these phenomena requires a phenomenological approach. In my own case, I borrow from my undergraduate major in comparative religion, and William James' classic *Varieties of Religious Experience* (1910) as a systematic study of everyday beliefs and practices. At the time I was studying, many of the research methods in comparative religion were phenomenological – emphasising the need to talk to people about their experiences, and develop systematic descriptions, rather than seek objective truth about the fundamental nature of religion.

As a result, my own research has focused on understanding varieties of programming experience (Blackwell and Fincher 2010). I am less interested in understanding the experiences of programming language designers, and more interested in understanding everyday experience – like the religion of people who speak English rather than the religion of people who speak Latin. In fact, there are two reasons why I think it is a bad idea to listen too much to the opinions of programming language designers – one academic, and one practical. The academic reason is that the people who design programming languages are easily able to speak for themselves, and in fact their views are quite widespread and influential, so it seems that I can deliver better academic value by saying different things from the rest of crowd.

The practical reason is a basic principle of good user interface design. A programming language is clearly a user interface – between the programmer and the compiler (or virtual machine). As with all user interface design work, the designer should remember that the user is not like them. Computer science students often make the mistake of assuming that users will know the things they know, and think the way they do. We explain to our students that this can't be true, because the designer understands internal details of the system that the user need never be aware of. More importantly, the equivalence set of computer science undergraduates is sufficiently small that this is not a very attractive market, so designing according to one's own needs and intuitions seems like a recipe for very small profits, or even market failure.

In the case of programming languages, most programming language inventors have deep knowledge of designing compilers and type checkers, and substantial experience of writing programs to implement such things. When they imagine what a *typical* programming task looks like, their imagination is often based on their personal experience – they think that typical programming tasks are like those involved in designing compilers and type checkers. In fact, this belief is not simply implicit – it is explicitly advocated, in the long-standing custom that a good test of a new language is to see whether it can compile itself. Unfortunately, the implication of my argument is that this is the *worst* test of a new language – if it can compile itself, this may be a sign that you have created a tool for other compiler writers, and possibly for nobody else.

Epilogue

So, if we were going to take a phenomenological approach to understanding the user experience of programming, and if we were going to make the strategic decision that the last people to listen to are the existing designers of programming languages, how should we go about that task? The results could be very significant, if we consider the next generation of programming languages in the light of the historical examples I have discussed. Perhaps we have a breakthrough on its way, comparable to the period when medieval Latin was abandoned for an everyday language of philosophy, or when mathematical gamesmanship was replaced with natural science of observation? The economic and commercial opportunities of vernacular programming certainly seem as profound today as in those past centuries – all we need is to see where they lie.

In some ways, programming language design seems like an old-fashioned branch of computer science. Excitable students and media commentators are under the impression that future computers will "teach themselves", or work out what to do through Turing-test equivalent dialog with human masters (or servants). My view is that Semiotic Engineering will continue to offer a critical perspective on the application of artificial intelligence and deep learning systems. Clarisse Sieckenius de Souza asks us to consider not simply how, but who it is that we are speaking with. The surface features of programming languages are constantly changing, whether rules, icons, labels, or virtual reality headsets. But always, there are people speaking. The rhetoric of technologists, and the commercial arrangements of technology corporations, may attempt to obscure this fact. But recognising computers as language systems is essential to a humane science of computing.

References

Blackwell AF, Fincher S (2010) PUX: patterns of user experience. Interactions 17(2):27–31

Eco U (1995) The search for the perfect language. Wiley, London

James W (1910) The varieties of religious experience: a study in human nature. Longmans Green and Company, New York

Kaijanaho AJ (2015) Evidence-based programming language design: a philosophical and methodological exploration. Jyväskylä studies in computing, p 222

Moody D (2009) The "physics" of notations: toward a scientific basis for constructing visual notations in software engineering. IEEE Trans Softw Eng 35(6):756–779

de Souza CS (2005) The semiotic engineering of human-computer interaction. MIT press, Cambridge, MA

de Souza CS, de Gusmão Cerqueira RF, Afonso LM, de Mello Brandão RR, Soares J, Ferreira J (2016) Software developers as users: semiotic investigations in human-centered software development. Springer, New York

Stajano F (2000) Python in education: raising a generation of native speakers. In: Proceedings of 8th international python conference

Warwick A (2003) Masters of theory: Cambridge and the rise of mathematical physics. The University of Chicago Press, Chicago. ISBN 0-226-87375-7

Semiotic Engineering – An Opportunity or an Opportunity Missed?

Mihai Nadin

Abstract Semiotics has to be understood as the conceptual undergirding of any form of design and engineering. While it does not provide operational means, it rather demands understanding of design and engineering aspects in a broad sense. Without the underlying semiotics, design and engineering remain mere problem-solving activities, and therefore will fall short of achieving their formative function. Through design, interaction languages, pertinent to engineering, contribute to shaping culture. In the end, semiotics contributes to making such languages available. The world before the computer and the world after the computer, including the ubiquitous smartphone, are not only technologically different, but also essentially culturally different. With the smartphone we progress from mere data processing to machine learning based interactive computation. The hybrid human-interactive computation has anticipatory characteristics.

Introduction

With the advent of the digital computer—in particular the embodiment of the Turing algorithmic machine in the von Neumann architecture—the notion of human-machine interaction took on a new dimension. The transition from a physical knob to the virtual (i.e., the interactive visual representation) was different from that experienced during former changes of interaction modalities. The lever did not need an interface: it was the extension of the human arm. Once it morphed into the pulley, it lost some of its immediateness and transparency: you needed to imagine an arrow that represented the place where force would be applied in order to lift a weight. In the progression of machines, the language of interaction became more elaborate. The clock—at one point the "poster image" for the machine—had a semiotic interface between the gears and pulleys and the user. This interface translated the gravitation-based measurement of intervals. It indexed how long it took a cause (gravitational attraction) to have an effect (the fall of a body, dead or alive).

M. Nadin (✉)
antÉ – Institute for Research in Anticipatory Systems, University of Texas at Dallas, Richardson, TX, USA
e-mail: nadin@utdallas.edu; https://www.nadin.ws

S.D.J. Barbosa, K. Breitman (eds.), *Conversations Around Semiotic Engineering*, DOI 10.1007/978-3-319-56291-9_6

Semiotics, in form of the clock face, created the illusion of time, much as today it creates the illusions of a variety of modeling and simulation applications. With the computer, the clock became a synchronizing mechanism. Of course, the digital display of time is quite different from that of the famous clocks (in the Old Town Square of Prague or the **Rathaus Glockenspiel in Munich**), associated with images of stars moving in cosmic space. You drive and the smartphone knows where you are through your coordinates in time and space, and what you are supposed to do and what not. During the night you'd better have your headlights on. Handwriting and driving are incompatible (day and night). And here you have *Deus ex Machina* taking care of you. The machine talks to you.

These preliminary illustrative remarks are intended as the background for the discussion of the extent to which semiotics, as we know it from de Saussure, Hjelmslev, Peirce et al. is significant and effective. Or if we need a better semiotics, adapted to the dynamics of human-machine interaction in the age of ever faster computations. More and richer interactions elicit better, i.e., adequate, semiotics. Most of the time, this is an implicit semiotics, to which designers and engineers have contributed—but not semioticians. Clarisse Sieckenius de Souza, who has remained dedicated to semiotic engineering, and who has been celebrated for her achievements, would argue that I am, if not wrong, at least not well informed. We always parted ways in our understanding of semiotics (see Nadin 2011), but not in the realization that semiotics is essential when approaching interactions with machines. For me, this opportunity to celebrate one of our own who practices semiotic engineering is not for restating incompatibilities, but rather for highlighting how her views, anchored in the semiotic system of natural language, eventually succeeded.

Believe it or not, ontology engineering—a field of extreme significance in the new phase of computation that recently began—is the victory *à rebours* (against the grain, we would say) of de Souza's semiotic engineering. Indeed, in our days, a dedicated group of computer scientists is practicing ontology engineering in order to "open access to meaning" (in a way of speaking, of course) to machines meant to do more than data processing. Like Sieckenius de Souza, the ontology engineers operate in the language domain; and what makes their effort so impressive is the algorithmic computation of the activity of building digital encyclopedias (some for medical applications, some for energy management, some for financial transactions, etc.). The focus is on knowledge processing, often understood by them as independent of our many forms of representation (words, sounds, images, media aggregates, etc.). For them an image is what we see. On the smartphone, an image is processed in the knowledge domain of visual expression.

Machines, among them algorithmic computers, operate at the syntactic level. Therefore, in order to tell them what we mean when we program them, using artificial languages, to execute a certain command, ontology engineers reach back to definitions that are *sui generis* ontologies, i.e., they describe the existent. They work, for instance, within predicate logic, which of course is not the same as the logic of vagueness, as Peirce defined his semiotics. The dedicated effort of ontology engineers led to Siri (a personal assistant), Cortana, S-Voice, Google Now, and the like (too many to be all mentioned, some better than the others). Voice Attack freed the hands of gamers looking for game immersiveness (the voice initiates keystrokes). None of these speech recognition utilities, interfaced with applications (e.g., the e-mail program or the weather prediction app), understands what it means when we ask a smartphone "to do" something. They translate (via databases, for example) what they do not understand, checking against accepted definitions (actual uses of the word), and utilizing computable functions for this purpose. This particular form of semiotic engineering is, at closer examination, as primitive as programming at the machine language level. But very effective. To argue with success is at best comical. Of course, if ontology engineers understood semiotics—John Sowa (2000) is trying hard to convince them—the entire effort would be more successful by many orders of magnitude. In line with this observation, one can continue by stating that the smartphone is really a "dumb phone," to which we attach, via ontology engineering, powerful semiotic functions facilitated by machine learning. Even if those who do that are most ignorant of semiotics most of the time. (Pat Hayes and his followers come to mind.) But let us not get to the end of the track before running a short marathon to prove the statements—as do those who never run, i.e. the commentators and critics, but are always ahead of everyone, the first to explain how they would have won! (As a practitioner of semiotics, Sieckenius de Souza would smile at this.) Having concretely applied semiotics (working for Apple's Lisa computer, or for IBM, Siemens, DaimlerChrysler on applications different from smartphones), I am, as much as she is, suspicious of those who claim credit for using semiotic terminology, without really understanding semiotics. This is a good place to sketch a possible genuine semiotic application as it pertains to the ubiquitous cellular phone elevated to the rank of smart device.

From the Analytical to the Generative Level

Semiotics can be a powerful analytical tool. It was already deployed in the evaluation of the interaction between a user and a machine, as well as in the evaluation of the interaction of machines. Nokia—for those who remember the innovative company from Finland—"knew" the value of semiotics. It used to conceive, design, and produce their mobile phones—75% was manufactured in their factories. Other companies used semiotics in the evaluation of process interfaces within a machine. In the particular case of computers, which are rather conceptual artifacts than physical machines, a variety of means can be deployed in order to facilitate the interactions between the human being and the particular digital device. Way back in the history of computation, means and methods pertinent to interaction with other machines were taken over and tested. A whole lot of knobs, sliders and dials were used in the first computers to help the user "tell" the machine what was expected. (Initially many military applications, in which targeting implied fine tuning, dominated.) In our days, Engelbart's "mouse"—nothing more than an interrupt device—in a variety of embodiments, is still present on the desktop with which uses interact via a language of visual commands. But other than that, the computer was emancipated from methods of physical control and tuning. Sutherland's pointer (one, the Sketchpad of 1963, dedicated to engineering tasks (Sutherland 1963)) and the touch screen (with a long history, going back to the 1970s) made anything that could be displayed (a pixel, an image) a potential "inter-face." The graphical user interface (famously known as GUI) replaced line commands. The history is sufficiently well known (Shneiderman 1983) so as not to be repeated here. However, *windows, icons, menus, pointer*—what became the WIMP paradigm, especially in personal computers— cannot be ignored when referring to the new devices that dominate our time. WIMP-based interactions use a virtual input device to control the visual space of commands, almost all compiled in menus. Actions can be performed even through gestures. A window manager, i.e., a semiotic interface, facilitates the interactions between windows and applications. Mobile devices, such as personal digital assistants (PDAs) and smartphones, use the WIMP elements with their own particular metaphors. Constraints in space, and especially the availability of sensors as input devices, led to a whole lot of new interaction techniques, labelled *post-WIMP* user interfaces. Touchscreen-based operating systems such as Apple's iOS (iPhone) and the Android use the post-WIMP class of GUIs. They support styles of interaction using more than one finger in contact with a display.

With or without semioticians (most of the time without), the computer morphed from forms of rudimentary interaction via interfaces to being a semiotic entity—representations of objects and actions made into effective forms of interacting with the machine. The smartphone is a rather elaborate artifact, in which the embedded sensors constitute interfaces to the world in which we live and work. Through sensors, users are positioned in space and referenced to a timeline. Moreover, in a mapped world—including its history (if we consider the pretty astonishing EarthTimeLapse™ just released by Google) we realize how the context changes. Even further, in a world of real stores, restaurants, schools, self-driving cars, etc., the interactive machine (no longer an algorithmic device!) becomes the locus of many transactions. Through sensors embedded in the wearable device, an individual is identified as a human in action (walking, running, playing games, cooking, typing, driving, and much more). In the digital world, the user is a "simile" of him/herself empowered to perform certain actions, but at the same time "incarcerated" in the world of competing opportunities. (The golden cage of the consumption economy!) If we take a strict sign-based semiotic perspective, the iPhone, or the Galaxy, or any competing brand (Blackberry, LG, Nokia, Huawei, etc.) can be seen as a sign—actually a supersign: a semiotic aggregate of a very large number of interrelated signs (Fig. 1).

In what follows, we will provide details of a possible analytic approach based on semiotics, independent of the smartphone manufacturer.

Fig. 1 Smartphones—a large variety of semiotic applications as means of identification and interaction with the user

Semiotics Applied to HCI – An Evaluation Tool

We already stated that within a sign-focused semiotics, the analytic dimension dominates. In other words, this is semiotics applied *after* the design and implementation, not as a guide to it.

HCI Is an Example of Peircean Semiotics at Work

The sign is the unity of what is represented (the object), how it is represented (the representamen), and the open-ended process of interpretation (the interpretant). Let us now examine the signs involved in HCI. In other words, how do we understand design interaction informed by semiotic awareness? Years back (Nadin 1988), when I introduced semiotics to those seeking some help in addressing the issue of human-computer interaction (at the tutorial *Interface Design, A Semiotic Paradigm*, Applications on the Leading Edge, 4th Annual Pacific Northwest Computer Graphics Conference, University of Oregon, Eugene, OR, October 27–29, 1985) is the first on record regarding the subject), the take was, although methodic, intuitive. The sign definition, adopted from C.S. Peirce guided the entire approach: A sign is something, *A*, which brings something, *B*, its *interpretant* sign determined or created by it, into the same sort of correspondence with something, *C*, its *object*, as that in which itself stands to *C* (Peirce 1902).

I do not wish to rehash the example I used at that time (working as consultant for Apple, focused on the machine called Lisa). Instead I shall take the smartphone as the new "patient" seeking advice from a "doctor specialized in HCI."

In human-computer interaction, we can consider the smartphone as the object (what is represented) and the operating system (choices are limited to Apple's proprietary OS, to Google's Android, BlackBerry, and to Microsoft Windows Phone) as the representamen. The desktop metaphor—appropriated from the semiotics-inspired icon-driven Xerox Star machine of 1981 to the Lisa (1984) and then to the Mac (and from there to every other machine)—is an example of a representamen. It stood for the office (files, folders, file cabinets, garbage can, etc.); and it stands today for the "housing" of applications (called *apps,* for the sake of abbreviation), ranging from text and data processing, to telecommunication (what used to be the function of a telephone), taking pictures and making videos, finding a location, calling up a service provider (such as the Uber or Lyft). The computer had a limited number of programs that performed desired functions. The smartphone is a social housing facility under siege. Everyone has a new app to offer—for banking, reading, interactive newspapers and magazines, music listening, movie watching, game playing, etc. Finally, the most important aspect is the deployment of apps (almost 80% of them are never or rarely used). A specific use—check blood pressure or cardiac rhythm, play a game, get a wake-up call, etc.—is a possible interpretation. In the act of doing something, which is the process of interpretation, the sign comes to life, acquiring meaning. Speech recognition is such an interpretation. Obviously, in such an interpretation (one application from many), a lot is left out—for instance, how speech commands turn into operations, how they call up associated programs, how learning (patterns of activity) take place. The smartphone is a not a mere computer with more functions and components (sensors, for example) than the desktop machine in the office. It became a smart typewriter that "understands" speech and drives a text processing program with associated layout functions and self-correction utilities (spelling, grammar, linking, etc.). Taking a picture (selfie or not) is also an interpretation from a very large number of possibilities associated with a digital camera, to which video and sound recording belong as well. Editing on the fly is also possible, as are various encodings and large file sharing.

The same smartphone offers its interpretation as a data-processing device, as a database management tool, and as a multimedia console. It can function as a game console, as a medical evaluation platform (communicating with the physician's office) based on the specific apps a user interacts with. By the same token, the object can be an application: Photoshop (the metaphor of the darkroom carried over to the digital realm), database, text processing, visualization, e-commerce, among other applications. The representamen is the "representation" of the "language" one must command in order to achieve the desired performance. And the interpretation is the performance actually achieved. Sign processes—also called *semioses* (singular: *semiosis*) in the jargon of semiotics—are nothing other than the coming to life of the manufactured piece of hardware enticing more and more users, facilitating richer and more creative interactions. Their use is semiotics at work—even if those who designed the device, those who made it, those who market it, those who provide the infrastructure for their networking, etc., never heard about semiotics (as is usually the case). As designed artifacts, smartphones are the output of an activity—to design—which means to express in signs (de-sign, as in visual representations of such a device). Ontology engineers actually focus on designing tasks and the level of conceiving new meaningful entities.

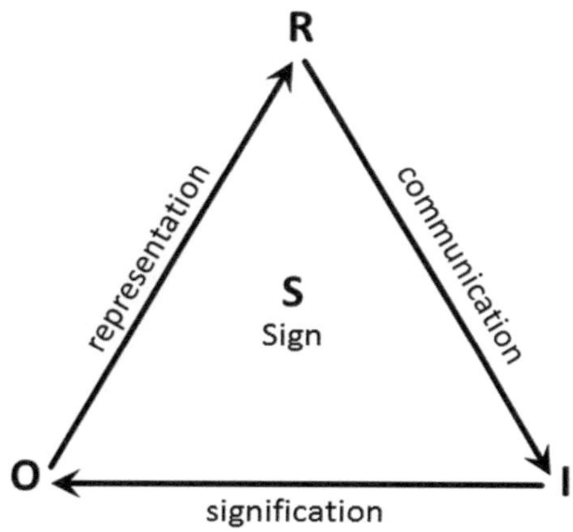

Fig. 2 The Smartphone as a sign: three semiotic functions define its future operations

One Sign – Three Functions

The unity of what is represented, how or through what that representation takes place (medium), and interpretation (the operation desired or actually performed, e.g., I want to process an image, write a letter, buy a car online, etc.) constitutes the sign. The three functions of the sign—representation, communication, and signification—can be understood only together (i.e., as an ensemble) (Fig. 2).

If we choose the smartphone to be considered as a sign, it will stand for the design through which it eventually became the smartphone—iPhone, Galaxy, Blackberry, etc. There is a lot of high technology to account for, but also a lot of interaction design. In this representation, the smartphone's aesthetic qualities are part of the semiosis. Remember when Apple sued Samsung for theft of aesthetic identity (the round corners, for example)? In reality, Apple is a marketing company: 189 suppliers, working at 789 locations, none owned by Apple, translate design specs into what became the success story known as iPhone. *Proprietary* refers to uniqueness, to protected means that give a product its edge over others. Smartphone manufacturers often use similar chips (such as those Samsung sells to Apple suppliers) and sensors, but almost never embody the same interaction specifications. Each generates its own space of potential meanings (Fig. 3).

Representation

A *caveat*: An unfortunate, simplified model of Peirce's semiotics (due mainly to Charles Morris, but since then adopted by many pseudo-semioticians) popularized three forms of representation—iconic, indexical, symbolic—as three different types of signs (Fig. 4). Removed from the context of sign definition, these forms are mistakenly called signs—even by practicing semioticians. Why do I say mistakenly? The error is evident. In respect to space, you cannot speak of volume, for instance,

Fig. 3 The "edge" of a competing smartphone. The Supreme Court of the USA involved in the dispute over claims of design and uniqueness (translated into money, which is a poor definition of their meaning)

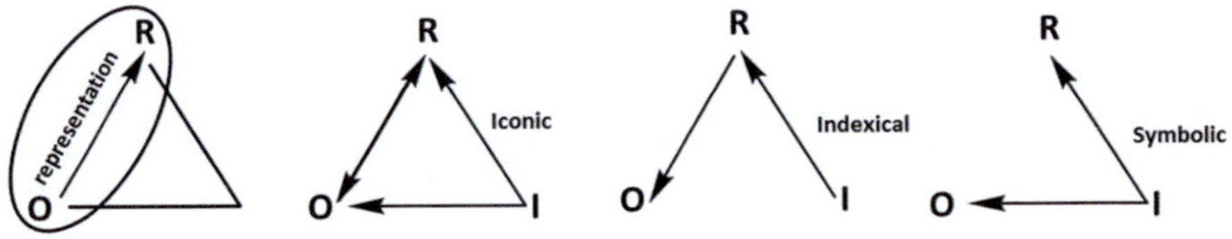

Fig. 4 The diagram explains the three distinct forms of representation (iconic, indexical, symbolic) characteristic of Peirce's semiotics

without acknowledging its three dimensions in the measurement. It is wrong to simply say that the volume of a room is five *square* yards (meters for non-USA readers); you need to define the three dimensions of volume: width, depth, height. Accordingly, it is just as wrong to say that a particular form of representation is a sign without identifying object, representamen, and interpretant. You cannot characterize a sign only by how it represents the object without relating to the other two aspects: the kind of representation and the kind of interpretant.

Let's progress from the definition level to the practical level. The actual embodiment of the smartphone is the representamen for the object represented by a computer endowed with many sensors and capable of interconnection (the post-WIMP mode of interaction). What kind of representamen is appropriate?

You have to relate characteristics of the object: WHAT is represented to HOW these characteristics are represented, and to their open-ended interpretation. Are we looking at an object's qualities (e.g., softness, color)? Are we looking at its necessary condition? (For example, water is necessarily the combination of hydrogen and oxygen; gravity will cause objects heavier than air to fall to Earth.) Are we focusing on its singular nature (i.e., unique, such as the uniqueness of each individual)? In the case of the smartphone, we could start at the intuitive level: make it pleasant, make it look like something we are familiar with. What should it be? The old telephone? Probably not. A circular form (like a big button)? A little animal? To find out what guides the decision making process of the designer, we need to define what is represented. The adopted form corresponds to studies in ergonomics (focused on what better fits in our hands) but makes possible variations (corresponding to individual characteristics, such as the difference in vision, left or right handedness, etc.).

What Is Represented?

In Peirce's semiotics, based on a broader view of what objects (including here actions) are, we deal with uniqueness, formal qualities, and necessary character. One is chosen as representative. For the sake of clarity, here is the diagram indicating the triadic-trichotomic structure of any sign—be it part of visual representations, actions, abstract signs, etc., or any other representation (e.g., sonification).

The diagram is self-explanatory: the object represented and the interpretation of the representation are connected. If we choose a certain characteristic of the object as relevant to the action performed, this characteristic is acknowledged in the representation. For all practical purposes, the smartphone is a larger post-it, good for writing notes, but also for storing information, manipulating it, and displaying it. Ideally, it should be customizable, and chances are good that this will eventually happen (Fig. 6).

Of course, before this should happen, we need to better understand what makes the sign definition necessary. I shall take each possibility defined in Fig. 5 (the triadic-trichotomic structure of the sign) and see how it applies to the smartphone (of course, this is more explanatory than procedural at this juncture).

Sin-sign Exemplified through a Signature—think of a password or a fingerprint—a sin-sign is an object of a singular nature. It can be imitated: you look at a signature and try to match the handwriting and the type of pen and ink used. When dealing with a signature, what you probably want is to make only one interpretation possible. For example, if someone wants to cash a check, the banker has to be sure that the signature of the endorser belongs to the appropriate person. If someone wants to access a file, that person should be entitled, and the HCI characteristic of the validation should be designed to make this clear to everyone: "Don't even try if you are

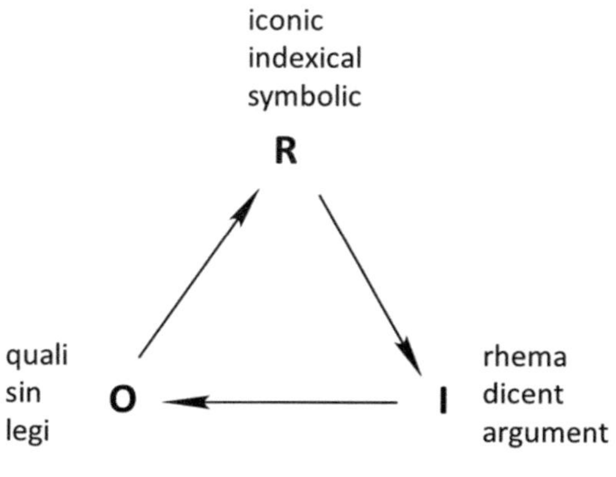

Fig. 5 The triadic-trichotomic structure of the Peirce-defined sign

Fig. 6 A future of customizable smartphones

not entitled!" On the smartphone, the sin-sign aspect (i.e., singularity) is very important: the device has to know in "whose hand" it is, i.e., whether that individual is entitled to use the many functions (including bank operations) or not. It actually learns to distinguish between the legitimate user and any other accidental users. In our days, when identity theft is so prevalent, smartphone identification is probably more important than other functions.

Quali-sign A certain quality (e.g., softness, friendliness, pinkness) of an object or an action might stand for the entire object. Let's say, the *smiley*: :). It suggests that the object or action semiotically identified through this quality supports an interaction that is "friendly" (easy to use). The design of such an element involves understanding how, from among many sign characteristics, one can be selected to stand for the entire object or action it represents. Apple made the quali-sign its branding trademark—the company is more a design corporation than a science and technology driven production facility. But typically quali-signs cannot be protected. This explains many of the imitations (from the desktop metaphor it took over from Xerox to the windows desktop and more recently to the smartphone designs) that follow in the company's footsteps.

Legi-sign The legi-sign says that *something has to take place*. If you triggered a shutdown procedure (on a PC, on a UNIX machine, or on a Macintosh), the semiotics of the process has to be simple and direct: no more and no less heavy than the semiotics of a switch (ON/OFF). Shutting down the smartphone, in no matter which of its many variations available in the market, is not a luxury. Battery life and power availability (when you need the smartphone most, it should be functional) are important considerations. Other actions that deserve the same attention: Does the "conversation" with Siri, S-Voice or Cortana, or Google Now end on its own? Does the use of the microphone or the recording device intelligently end and reconvene when necessary? These are only two examples of questions that need to be addressed.

Important: the three aspects of the object are independent and not reducible one to another. But at times we would like to have all of them represented in the sign because each has a different role to play during use. It is at this level that semiotics becomes critical: how to establish a hierarchy of aspects when resources are limited, moreover when the awareness of the user's ability to navigate the huge space of possibilities becomes a major issue. The choice is also informed by the type of representations that will be used.

How Do We Represent? Indexically? Iconically? Symbolically?

Semiotic awareness involves understanding the different characteristics of the object or action represented. It also involves understanding the types of representation: indexical, iconic, symbolic. Please take note: These are types of representation, not types of signs. I explained this aspect in reference to the Lisa computer, on whose semiotic evaluation I worked. For the sake of clarity, I will repeat the visual argument as it pertains to the calculator omnipresent on computers and smartphones (Fig. 7).

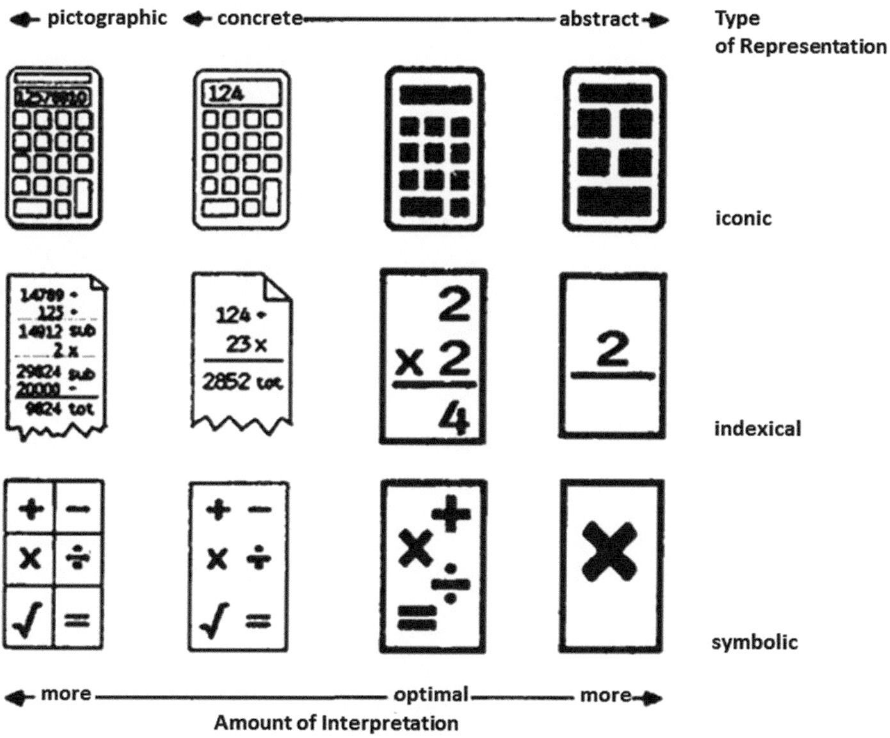

Fig. 7 Types of representation adequate to the desktop

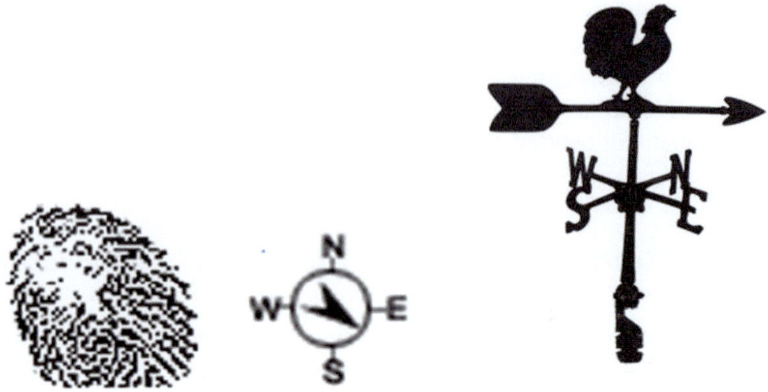

Fig. 8 Examples of indexical representations: fingerprint, compass, weathervane

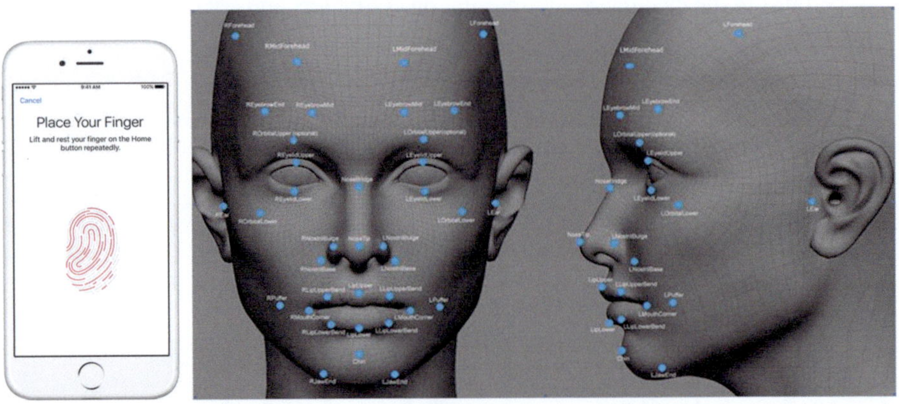

Fig. 9 The indexical fingerprint; face recognition as unique identifier

Indexical: The Marks Left by an Object

The definition is important for understanding that a language of interaction will have to provide integrated indexical signs. On the smartphone, the fingerprint is now a feature (payment via the smartphone is one application where the fingerprint is used) (Figs. 8 and 9).

There is also the smartphone with eye scanners—not really convenient enough in order to be accepted—or biometric fingerprint scanners—where convenience also suffers. Recently, as augmented reality (AR) makes it into the app world of smartphones, facial recognition is offered as a feature. Semiotically, these alternatives are valid; but in the end it depends on the degree to which the additional security justifies the overhead in operations to achieve such security.

Iconic: Resemblance to an Object

The famous garbage can icon became part of our visual language decades ago. I shall not forget the experience I had with Steve Jobs. The garbage can on Lisa came with a slant lid on it. Explaining to the mercurial manager why a slant lid was not necessary proved to be an exercise in futility ("Lisa likes it with a lid!"—Lisa was Jobs' girlfriend at that time). Jobs took a long time to understand the significance of semiotics. Paul Rand, the famous graphic designer who worked on the NeXT computer identity, helped in the process. He understood the value of semiotics. On many smartphones, if not a slanted lid, some other awkward icons populate the iconic world, making the interpretation more difficult (Fig. 10).

Let me add one example from the smartphone universe: In the Apple world, there is the wastbasket; on the Windows side, a recycle bin. On the Android smartphones, the "dumping" of data takes a different approach. The user is asked whether the data should be erased or not. This is, of course, a different semiotics. In reality, the iconicity is no longer meaningful, but since there is a "culture" of the operation of discarding data (files of all kind), designers build upon it (Fig. 11).

Fig. 10 Lisa computer trash can with useless lid

Fig. 11 Iconic variations

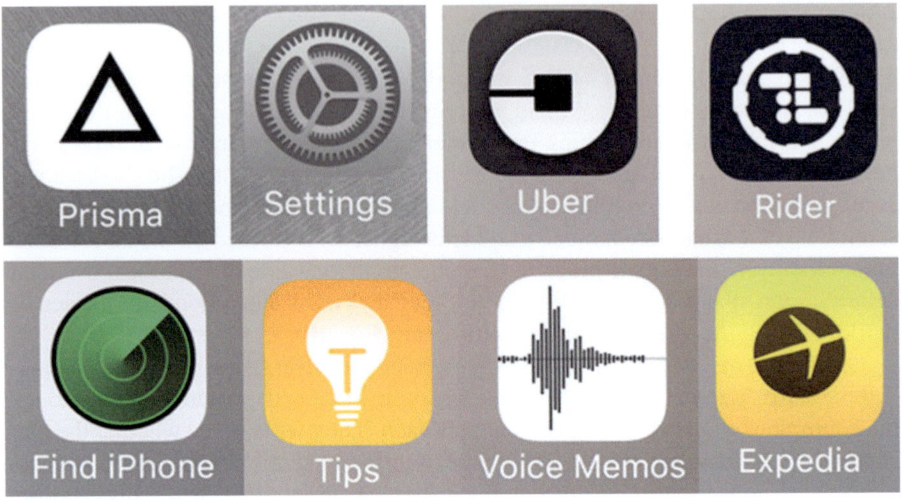

Fig. 12 The symbolic is the dominant form of representation

Symbolic

Example: in the convention of numerals (Roman, Arabic) standing for quantities: I, II, III, IV…; 1, 2, 3, 4.... To be clear: most of the time, we are in the symbolic representation domain. We share the meaning of most of our representations: words (which stand for objects), symbols, sounds, etc. The smartphone is the symbolic aggregate of many represented objects and actions. In the end, what distinguishes the various embodiments of the smartphone is the symbolic domain, i.e., the language of representations and actions they facilitate (Fig. 12).

Interpretant Process. Or Sign Closure

In other words: What do we do with such devices? This is the goal of the entire attempt to consider the semiotics of the smartphone (or any other device we conceive of or use). We can now combine what is represented and how it is represented.

What: the place where we dispose of what we do not need or desire. What we represent is neither a unique characteristic nor a singular characteristic.

How: It is most commonly represented iconically. It looks like a wastebasket. But it can be represented symbolically, in the action called Erase/Throwaway/Discard.

However, the semiotics of the interaction makes sense only in the context of its specific use. Based on my evaluation of smartphones, this is the weakness of almost every device I had in my hands. The awareness of context, made possible by sen-

Fig. 13 Representations are interpreted. The pragmatic aspect of GUI

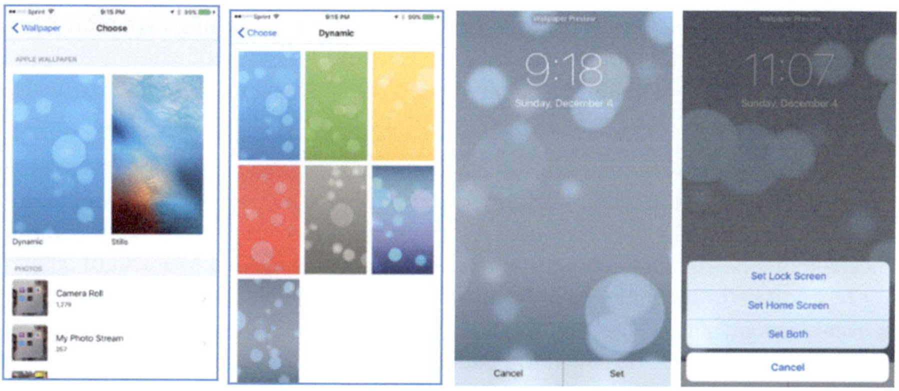

Fig. 14 Individualizing the smartphone—still a rudimentary understanding of the pragmatics of individualized use

sors, is ignored in the design. The smartphone always appears as cluttered, way too busy, regardless of what we do with it. It is evident that smartphone designers are rarely aware of the semiotic principles according to which less is more. The user usually fills in the missing, the suggested.

Interpreting the Interpretant

Semiotic awareness necessitates defining a desired interpretation (Fig. 13): the "Aha!"—the taking notice of something, the awareness of the consequences of our actions (such as with the ERASE function), and the possibility of individualizing available possibilities (customization as an advanced interpretation) (Fig. 14).

As opposed to the reactive model of usability tests (addressing "which user," "the statistical average," "the focus group"), semiotics suggests the possibility of achieving semiotic adequacy. This is the interplay among various kinds of signs (visual, verbal, tactile, etc.) (Fig. 15), that is, the sign process conceived with a clear cognitive goal and evaluated in cognitive terms: proactive as opposed to the reactive usability measurements.

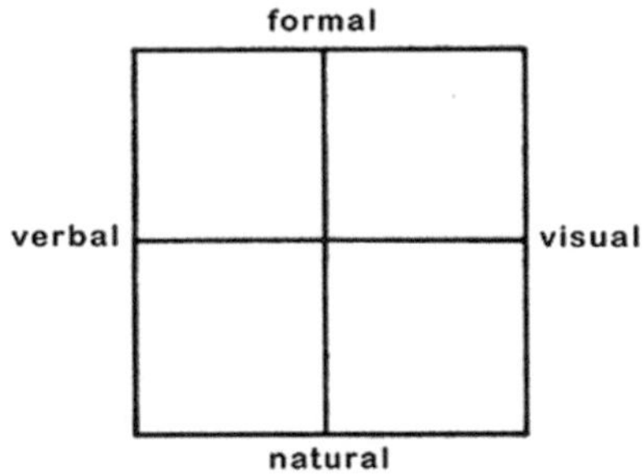

Fig. 15 The various languages of representation. Sonification, the new kid on the block, is making progress

Rhema: a realization—the Aha! effect of something we realize spontaneously, such as the iconic representation of the garbage can. Once in use, things get a bit more complicated. On the Macintosh desktop, one could take the icon of a floppy disk and place it in the garbage can! The result was the Eject function, semiotically inadequate, but which, through use, became part of the Macintosh "language."

Dicent: the calculator as an "icon" on the iconic interface. You use the representation of buttons as you would work with real buttons. This second level of iconic representation is a description of a description, etc. Semiotically, it is a primitive concept. But once computers without keyboards emerged (the great IBM Aha! Moment of attaching typewriters to computers), it proved to be quite an efficient means for HCI on pocket-sized gadgets. The virtual keyboard, available when needed, is the continuation for inputting text. So is the microphone, for speech commands.

On the smartphone, this tendency is usually abused. When youngsters have their thumbs surgically reshaped in order to play better, something is clearly wrong with how we make interactions with the device possible. Voice Attack is an inspired alternative. Given the potential of interactive computation, it becomes a challenge to the design and semiotic community to go beyond the icon of icon to new representations, probably embodied in some simple hardware interaction devices. The pen is one good example, although not always properly understood. The microphone, mentioned above, is yet another choice.

Argument: the level at which computations result from their own knowledge domain (visualization, simulation, etc.). Computational sciences are not some discourse about computers (including mathematics and logics), but are expressed in computational form. The HCI of this domain no longer limits itself to applications, but becomes part of the computation. Here HCI is dynamic, growing with the computational inquiry, and becomes part of the result. The entire area of adaptive interfaces (to which the gestural belongs) is a good example for this semiotic level. The smartphone definitely leads the development in this area.

Semiotic Adequacy

Semiotic means of all kinds are integrated in the process we call HCI—regardless whether pertinent to supercomputers, neural networks, or smartphones.

Machine learning improved not only speech recognition (around 4% margin of error), but also image recognition. In the sound domain, progress is even more impressive.

In order to evaluate the result of semiotic choices (what kind of semiotic processes should be considered) and the effectiveness of the semiosis we designed, we need to "run" the HCI "program," not unlike the way we test various software solutions. Adequacy is a qualitative measurement—it is focused on meaning. Semiotic adequacy is established through basic semiotic operations.

Substitution, i.e., variation of the representamen: the photographic camera shutter replaced by the image of an eye (Fig. 16).

Insertion, i.e., an addition of representamina (plural of representamen) until the object is adequately represented: horizontal reference and indicator of functioning (Fig. 17).

Omission, i.e., leaving aside or removing sign interpretations that obscure the semiosis. In one example, the arrow is removed but the subsequent change of function is indicated; in the second, indicator of functioning, dial, and horizontal index are omitted (Fig. 18).

Fig. 16 Example of substitution

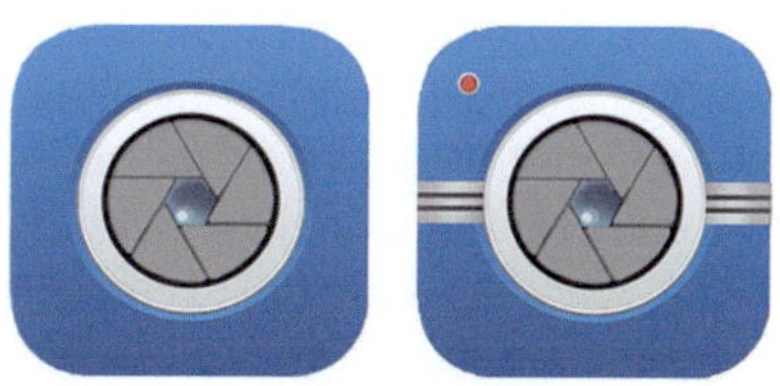

Fig. 17 Example of insertion

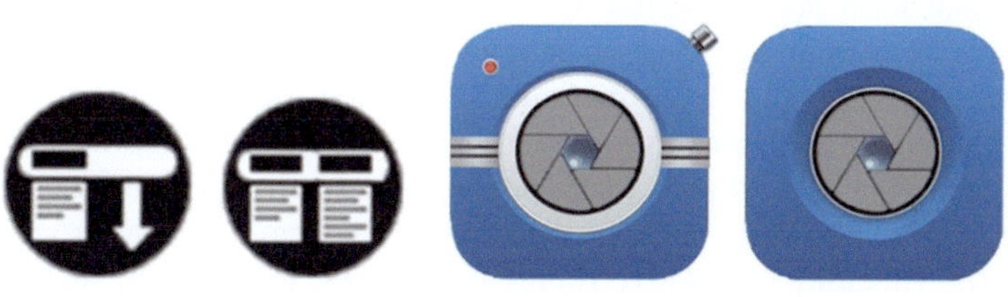

Fig. 18 Example of the semiotic operation of omission

Of course, these examples are more illustrations of how semiotic operations (insertion, substitution, omission) can be systematically pursued in order to optimize the interaction.

As opposed to the reactive model of measuring user performance—which is still the dominant evaluation method—semiotic adequacy is a method of fine tuning the semiotic elements involved in HCI. Adequacy reflects individual choices and can inform design decisions in the direction of individualization.

Aspects of Communication

The smartphone is the result of the progression of the morphing of the telephone and the computer: landline and connected device, mobile phone (a phone with an emitter and receiver at the end), cellular phone (part of an interconnected world of cells), and smartphone—a work still in progress. Around 2.5 billion smartphones are in use in our days; their number will double within the next 10 years. 60% of all time spent online in the USA involves the smartphone. The category of devices called personal assistants (PDA)—mobile units of all kind, functioning as personal information managers (some with phone functions integrated)—are different in nature from smartphones but related to them in terms of the technology used. Each of them is meant to support an intuitive interaction between user and device, i.e., straightforward communication. And each involves more and more machine learning—the capabilities associated with adaptive functions. Instead of requesting the user to perform certain operations, they detect patterns, they make inferences, and often reproduce desired operations. Let us examine here only the variety of situations occurring in the smartphone or PDA computation:

(a) The user and the smartphone/PDA in problem-solving interaction: let's say the SCAN application. The image of the document will eventually become a word-processed file that can be further used in other integrated functions.
(b) The smartphone/PDA and the user in an interaction focused on what is computable and what is not. We can get weather reports on the device, but we cannot process data associated with weather prediction. (For this type of application, supercomputers are still necessary.) The same holds true for earthquakes. But given machine learning, the device can associate data from weather centers and suggest levels of danger.
(c) Communication of results: the outcome of smartphone computation can take the form of commands, such as remote control of appliances in a home, for instance; or the form of data for training a neural network; or the information (data associated with meaning) underlying forms of learning. Indeed, applications extending into AI are rapidly spreading into smartphone uses. Examples related to medical diagnostic, to diagnostic in general (what's wrong with my car?), to evaluating alternative routes in logistics, to selecting stocks or other investment possibilities, are no longer an exception.

Semantics vs. Pragmatics

The smartphone is a very good example for understanding all the effort put in to achieve the semantic level of communication. When Sieckenius and her group refer to the specific aspects of how well designed some communicative aspects of a pull-down menu are, she makes us aware of the fact that semantics plays an important role. On the smartphone, the pull-down menu (still available) is not really progress. We'd better start looking into distributed means of communication to replace the tree structure in use today.

On the smartphone, more than on the Internet, users can define their goals without having translated meaning ("I want Sicilian pizza!") into the garble of syntactic approximations. This is, after all, the goal of ontology engineers. And they delivered. Communication is a theme of semantics; syntax refers to representation. Pragmatics integrates expression, representation, and communication and results in knowledge. Indeed, meaning—what we do is the result of seeking meaning in our activity— is the domain in which computation—most certainly not in algorithmic form—will eventually mature. At that time, we will no longer deal with devices, but with cognitive energy as a resource (similar to the electric energy—the Mark Weiser metaphor from 1993—*The world is not a desktop*—discussed in (Nadin 1997)). Designing Agency, as Lockton suggested—involving *Veronica Ranner, Gyorgyi Galik, Delfina Fantini van Ditmar, and Laura Ferrarello* in his argument (Lockton 2015)—*sounds good, but is more* suggestive *of what computation might one day become than* directional. *In reality, through devices accepting a rich variety of sensor input, the user becomes part of a hybrid human-machine entity: human intelligence and the facility to process data as the situation (context) requires. Sometime huge amounts of information (such as in financial analysis), other times small amounts of information, but significant. And most of the time very fast processes. The semiotics of such hybrid entities is a challenge that transcends technical feasibility.* However, semiotics becomes relevant only if the perspective is pragmatic: Why do we enter into interaction with a computer? Based on this assessment, we can define the semantics of HCI and design based on a syntax that allows for a clear "language" of interactions.

The task of semiotic engineering in respect to the smartphone—a step in the direction of ubiquitous computing—goes beyond what semiotics, in the sense it is practiced today, can actually provide. Users do not want "computerese," i.e., complicated operations and a lot of memorized commands, between them and the service they need. Here is where semiotics can be of immediate help. There is no doubt that the sign-based semiotics documented above could be a powerful analytical tool, but it will not help in doing away with the "in-between," (i.e. buttons, commands, monitors, etc.) of users and machines. Not very much semiotic competence is needed to take note of the fact that smartphones are the success story of a technology to which semiotics contributed close to nothing—Nokia was impatient when it got rid of its semiotics experts. Most of the time, the iconic interface of the desktop expanded into this new world of interactions. Nevertheless, the failure of semiotics in respect to the design of the smartphone is actually its opportunity.

In order to remain viable, semiotics must remain focused on meaning—which in the end is the reason why devices such as smartphones are used. They enable human activities not possible without them. Just think about a real-time navigation system, about social interaction, about new forms of monitoring health, finances, etc.; about staying connected to the world in whatever form one might wish; about a very rich assortment of peer-to-peer transactions. Traditional business models compete with real-time shared services. New efficiencies are facilitated through the smartphone. They help in overcoming handicaps, as well as in the effort to augment interaction. With smartphones, even relying on ontology engineering (covering for semiotics), the syntactic level of computation was transcended. The interconnected smartphone is a medium for richer forms of pragmatic expression, for human self-constitution through activities never before possible. The future hybrid entity—the human-interactive computer—uniting the living and data processing, is pragmatically relevant and becomes necessary on account of its pragmatic dimension.

A Challenge to Semiotics

I have argued in favor of a new foundation for semiotics (Nadin 2012), one that builds upon what we know about the sign, but which focuses on semiotic dynamics, not on sign typology. Sign and sign theories as we know them (de Saussure, Peirce, etc.) are no longer adequate for engineering meaningful semiotic experiences. The level at which these take place is that of the time series; that is, sequences of signs making up a real-time narrative. As such, these narrations—how to perform operations, how to integrate applications—constitute quite a number of interrelated languages, each with a precise focus, and all together able to reach expressivity.

Medicine, which is one of the activities within which semiotics emerged—just think about symptoms and the art and science of diagnostics—is a good example of why narration and story became necessary. It is also pretty much related to how the smartphone became an unavoidable link in what is called *eMedicine*. There are quite a number of parallel streams of data—such as blood pressure, heart rate, body temperature. And there are physiological data—such as cholesterol and glucose levels, blood count, creatinine, bilirubin, etc. The aggregate expression, that is, what physicians would interpret as the health condition, abnormalities, or deficiencies, is the meaningful story. Indeed, the narrations represented by the streams of data make up the story to be associated with means and methods for healing or correcting imbalances. There is the analytical level: establish the condition at a certain moment in time (identified in the narration). And there is an anticipatory dimension: what can and should be done to avoid the story called obesity, hypertension, type-2 diabetes, lower back pain, dyspepsia, or any of the maladies that can be prevented.

Take the example of how sequences of signs (the streams of data) become the narration for a medical condition and, when interpreted by the physician, result in

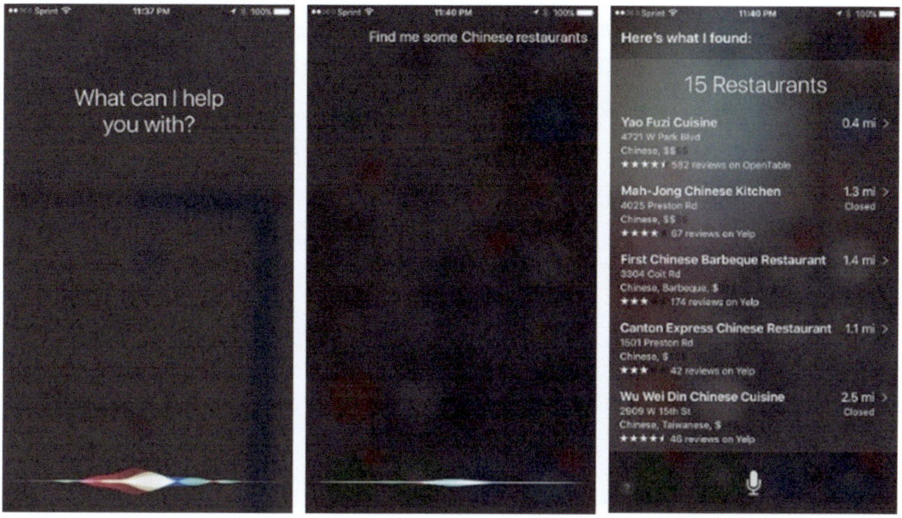

Fig. 19 Ontology engineering makes possible a pseudo-semantic level of interaction. Of course, the device does not know what a restaurant is and even less what a Chinese restaurant means

the story (e.g., diabetes means a metabolic disease in which the body's inability to produce any or enough insulin causes elevated levels of glucose in the blood). Apply this understanding of semiotics to the human-computer hybrid for which we chose the example of the smartphone. There are parallel and concurrent streams of data, afforded either by sensors or interactions (local or through the network). To proceed with the search for a jazz concert in town, to reserve tickets, to find a ride (with a friend, with Uber, or with the subway), and to frame the music played within your memory of similar events and, finally, to share it would make up the story of smartphone-supported activity. We can already address the digital assistant (Fig. 19).

Another example refers to performing certain operations, which on hardware devices (such as video cameras) were pre-determined in the material components (gears, speed control, etc.). With the smartphone, we can produce a slow-motion image (Fig. 20) by following a sequence of commands (the syntax of the operation) and expecting other commands, such as the slower motion effect, to be executed by the device.

Using an app such as Office Lens, we can take an image and generate a document, or even a whiteboard. The user-computer hybrid is involved in some of the operations. The rest is performed according to specifications corresponding to our experience with certain activities (Fig. 21).

Essential is the understanding that in this new phase of semiotic engineering, we conceive of effective interaction language. Interfacing among various integrated functions means, after all, reaching the pragmatic level of semiotics. There was never a better time for ascertaining the need for semiotics in a world where way too often we focus on data but fail to realize the meaning of what we do. Anticipatory characteristics, reflecting the individuality of each person, become possible within the frame of interactive computation.

Fig. 20 The syntax of the operation of filming in slow motion integrates button operations not related to the activity

Fig. 21 A complete design procedure is the result of integrating the semiotics of the layout. This in itself is a visual language

References

Lockton D (2015) Let's see what we can do: designing agency, December 2015, https://www.medium.com

Nadin M (2011) Information and semiotic processes. The semiotics of computation (review article). In: Pearson C (guest ed); Brier S, et al. (eds) Cybernetics and human knowing. A journal of second-order cybernetics, autopoiesis and cyber-semiotics, 18:(1–2), 153–175

Nadin M (1988) Interface design and evaluation. In: Hartson R, Hix D (eds) Advances in human-computer interaction, vol 2. Ablex Publishing, Norwood, pp 45–100

Nadin M (2012) Reassessing the foundations of semiotics: preliminaries. Int J Signs Semi Syst 2(1):1–31

Nadin M (1997) The civilization of illiteracy. Dresden University Press, Dresden

Peirce CS (1902) On the definition of Logic, New Elements of Mathematics, 4: 20–21. (See also: https://inquiryintoinquiry.com/2012/06/01/c-s-peirce-%E2%80%A2-on-the-definition-of-logic/

Shneiderman B (1983) Direct manipulation: a step beyond programming languages. IEEE Computer 16(8):57–69

Sowa JF (2000) Knowledge representation: logical, philosophical, and computational foundations. Brooks Cole Publishing Co., Pacific Grove

Sutherland IE (1963). Sketchpad. A man-machine graphical communications system. Submitted in partial fulfillment of the requirements for the degree of doctor of Philosophy, Massachusetts Institute of Technology, January 1963

Semiotic Engineering as Teaching

Allen Cypher

Abstract I was fortunate to learn Semiotic Engineering directly from Prof. de Souza when she was a Visiting Scholar at the IBM Almaden Research Center in California in 2007. We took the opportunity to apply the principles of Semiotic Engineering to the redesign of the CoScripter system that I was researching at the time. We published the results of our investigation as "Semiotic Engineering in Practice: Redesigning the CoScripter Interface" (de Souza CS and Cypher A, Semiotic engineering in practice: redesigning the CoScripter interface. In: Proceedings of the working conference on Advanced visual interfaces (AVI'08). ACM, New York, pp 165–172. doi: http://dx.doi.org/10.1145/1385569.1385597, 2008).

CoScripter

CoScripter is a system for sharing "how-to" knowledge about activities in a web browser. It consists of an extension to the Firefox web browser (Fig. 1) and an associated wiki website. The extension enables users to record their actions in the browser as scripts: when the "record" feature is *turned* on, CoScripter records a script of every action performed in Firefox—every click, every menu selection, and any command keys or text that are typed. CoScripter can then replay this script, performing all of the clicks, commands, and typing automatically. These recorded scripts are stored on a public wiki, so that all users can replay scripts created by others.

Scripts can be used to automate many tasks, such as filling in forms. An important feature of CoScripter is that commands are recorded in a language that (1) users are able to understand and (2) the computer is able to execute. This means that scripts can be used as a kind of "how-to" knowledge: as CoScripter replays actions, it highlights each action on the screen, turning buttons and links green as it clicks on them, and typing green text into text boxes. That way, users who have never performed a particular task can learn by watching the script as it executes.

A. Cypher (✉)
Socratic Arts, Stuart, FL 34996, USA
e-mail: acypher@acypher.com

S.D.J. Barbosa, K. Breitman (eds.), *Conversations Around Semiotic Engineering*, DOI 10.1007/978-3-319-56291-9_7

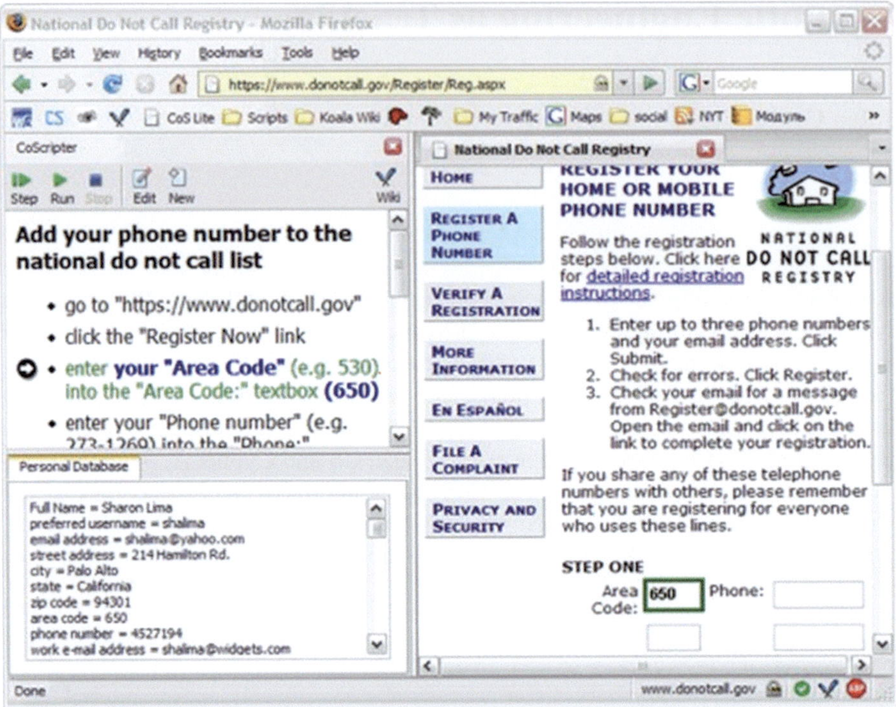

Fig. 1 CoScripter performing the third step in a script

Semiotic Engineering

As de Souza explained it, there are four fundamental concepts in semiotic engineering that are essential for UX designers to understand: Signs, Abduction, Resignification, and Meta-communication.

Signs A *sign* has three components: a *representation*, a *meaning*, and a *referent*. For instance, CoScripter has a "record" button, which is a *sign*. Its *representation* is 

. Its *meaning* is obtained by the user's familiarity with the red light that is used conventionally on physical tape recorders. Its *referent* is that "CoScripter is currently recording".

Abduction Peirce's concept of *abduction* (Peirce 1992) refers to the hypothetical reasoning that people use to make plausible inferences from the world around them—in particular, to determine the meaning of the signs in an interface. Noting that a red circle is similar to the recording light on physical tape recorders is an instance of abduction.

Resignification (aka Repurposing) The signification system in an interface will likely trigger a variety of interpretations in the user. Invariably, some of a user's interpretations will not coincide with the designer's intention. While these can lead to interaction failures, they can also lead to felicitous repurposing, and increased applicability of the software to uses that were not anticipated by the designer. I find it interesting that this is similar to the "Intentional Fallacy" in literary theory (Authorial Intent), which posits that the intent of the author is irrelevant to the meaning of a work of literature.

Meta-communication When a designer creates an interface composed of signs (i.e. a "signification system"), those signs actually serve two purposes. Primarily, they are used to perform actions in the interface. But secondarily, they are the only means available to the designer to communicate design intentions to the user.

Semiotic Engineering as Teaching

Some of the most important understandings that I took away from my work with Prof. de Souza involve this secondary role of meta-communication, and the insights that semiotic engineering affords into the practice of teaching.

Semiotic engineering applies the concept of abduction to user interface design through the principle that "A good designer tries to anticipate her users' abductions". I find great value in applying this principle to all forms of teaching. In order to teach a subject, all teachers need to first understand the subject matter themselves. This means that they formulate a coherent and self-consistent understanding of the subject. Next, in order to teach this subject, they must perform the task of converting their thoughts into words. Some teachers may be satisfied when they reach the point where they can clearly express, in words, this self-consistent understanding of their subject matter.

What distinguishes good teachers from ordinary teachers is the ability to go a step further and imagine what it will be like for their audience to hear those words. The good teacher imagines the experience of the listener trying to understand those words, and appreciates that the process that her listeners will go through while interpreting and attempting to understand those words will necessarily differ from the process that she went through in creating the words. The good teacher imagines the preconceptions and related conventions that will be triggered in her listeners, and notes where those triggered thoughts will lead the listener to make incorrect interpretations. She can then go back and revise her verbalization until she feels confident that it will trigger thoughts that lead her listeners to the desired interpretation and understanding.

Semiotic Engineering provides a precise vocabulary and precise concepts for characterizing these qualities of a good teacher. The good teacher anticipates the abductions of her audience, and the resulting resignifications that lead to incorrect conclusions.

Software designers are in a situation very similar to teachers, and it is precisely for this reason that the stance taken by semiotic engineering is so vital to the software designer. The good interface designer attempts to anticipate the abductions of her users. This understanding is essential to creating an understandable interface. When it is likely that the user's abduction will lead to a misunderstanding (a "communicative failure"), the designer goes back to the drawing board.

With this understanding of why "A good designer tries to anticipate her users' abductions", we are now ready to analyze the design of the Record Button.

The original design of CoScripter turned on Recording as soon as the user clicked the button to begin creating a new script. The designers had two good reasons for this. (1) Most users would turn on Recording themselves as soon as they started a new script, and (2) It was important for new users to see recording in action as soon as possible.

Furthermore, the designers selected a "glowing red button with the word Record underneath" as the symbol for "CoScripter is now recording", based on the convention from physical tape recorders where a physical red light glows while the device is recording (Fig. 2).

These are all reasonable justifications, and they would be good messages for the designers to communicate to their users. However, in this particular case, this message was not compellingly communicated due to the paucity of the interface. The sidebar in a web browser is necessarily a constricted space, so its signification system is necessarily constrained. And, even more importantly, the designers did not go through the process of anticipating the abductions that their design would induce in their users. Specifically, some users applied the convention of Occam's Razor: the simplest explanation must be the correct one. Similarly, one of Kurt VanLehn's "felicity conditions" for teaching is that only one new concept be introduced at a time (VanLehn 1983). Since the button that they pressed was labeled New, there was no reason for new users to expect that it would also perform the action of Record. Secondly, the designers also made the design decision to remove buttons from the display whenever they are not relevant (in order to conserve space), but this means

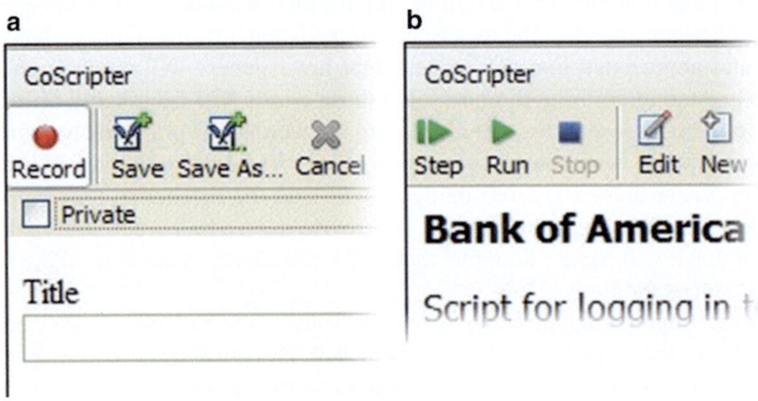

Fig. 2 (**a**) The record button while recording a script. (**b**) The buttons for running a script

that new users have never seen the off state of the Record button when it first appears. Without the 'off' state for comparison, it is unclear that the icon for the 'on' Recording state is actually meant to appear to be glowing.

This semiotic engineering analysis of the signification system that was chosen by CoScripter's designers illuminates difficulties in communicating the designer's message. We should add that in CoScripter's user studies, and in direct informal observation of novice users, some users failed to get the designer's message: they would click on the record button to 'start recording' their first script, which instead causes the system to stop recording (and brings about all sorts of subsequent communicative breakdowns in the interface). One user study participant said: "Well, I can't tell if it is pressed. Is that red telling me that I have to press it, or that I should press it? Or that it is recording?" These problems could have been avoided through a semiotic engineering analysis at design time.

Having been involved in User Centered Design and cognitive engineering since its inception (Cypher 1986), it was both challenging and exhilarating to learn the complementary theory of Semiotic Engineering. Like other theories of HCI design—such as Activity Theory, Participatory Design and Distributed Cognition—Semiotic Engineering affords a unique perspective that alerts designers both to unseen problems and to possible solutions.

References

Authorial intent https://en.wikipedia.org/wiki/Authorial_intent

Cypher A (1986) The structure of users' activities. In: Norman D, Draper S (eds) User centered system design. Lawrence Erlbaum Associates, Hillsdale, pp 243–263

de Souza CS and Cypher A (2008) Semiotic engineering in practice: redesigning the CoScripter interface. In: Proceedings of the working conference on advanced visual interfaces (AVI'08). ACM, New York, p 165–172. doi: http://dx.doi.org/10.1145/1385569.1385597

Peirce CS (1992, 1998) The essential Peirce: selected philosophical writings. vols I, II. Houser N and Kloesel CJW (eds). Bloomington. Indiana University Press

VanLehn K (1983) Felicity conditions for human skill acquisition: validating an AI- based theory, PARC Reports

Generative Art: A Semiotic Exchange

Ernest A. Edmonds

Abstract This chapter consists of an exchange between Clarisse Sieckenius de Souza and myself, the author, in which Clarisse posed a number of challenging questions about my art, the role of computer code, predictability and the essence, or locus, of the work from a semiotic perspective. The artworks of mine that the exchange deals with are generative, that is they are time-based and the way that they develop is determined by rules specified in a computer program, or, in addition, they are interactive. The first section provides the background to my work that puts the exchange in context, the second section provides the challenges from Clarisse and then third is my response.

Background

In 2015 I was part of an exhibition of four "pioneers" of computer-based art, *Códigos Primordiais (Primary Codes)* at Oi Futuro Flamengo in Rio de Janeiro. My fellow exhibitors were Harold Cohen, Frieder Nake and Paul Brown. A few images from the show, including my work, are shown in Figs. 1, 2 and 3. As well as presenting the artworks we gave talks at a panel discussion held in Oi Futuro on 19th June 2015. So we had public discussion about our works. Professor Clarisse Sieckenius de Souza was there and it was from that discussion that the exchange recorded in this paper arose. For a fuller background, I will explain some things about my work, recording some of the remarks that I made in Rio.

My work is abstract and minimal with a strong concern for colour. But, most relevant to this article is my strong interest in the use of software as a medium: a use that has evolved over nearly five decades. This discussion is concerned with issues relating to all of this work, but centres on my 21st Century developments and the *Shaping Form/Space* series of works (Edmonds, 2007). The *Shaping Form/Space*

E.A. Edmonds (✉)
Institute of Creative Technologies, Los Angeles, CA 90094, USA

Leicester Media School, De Montfort University, Leicester, UK
e-mail: ernest@ernestedmonds.com

S.D.J. Barbosa, K. Breitman (eds.), *Conversations Around Semiotic Engineering*, DOI 10.1007/978-3-319-56291-9_8

Fig. 1 Two *From Shaping Space* paintings, Ernest Edmonds 2012/2015

series consists of unique abstract interactive artworks that are each generating colours and forms in time from a set of unique rules: rules that are rather like their DNA. They also take data from a camera and continuously calculate the amount of activity seen in front of the work. The computer software then steadily modifies the rules. The people who look at it influence the artwork and its development over time. These are generative works that are changed by the influence of the environment around them. People can readily detect the immediate responses of the work to movement but the changes over time are only apparent when there is more prolonged, although not necessarily continuous, contact with it. The *Shaping Form/Space* represents computed life, moving and changing of its own accord but maturing and developing as a result of the movement of audiences. The installation *Shaping Space* is seen in a darkened room, two changing images create a field of colour, developing into a living matrix of colours that sometimes change very slowly and at other times burst into life.

As I explained in a 2003 paper (Edmonds, 2003), generative art was first seen as algorithmic, i.e. art produced with the aid of a computer by programming it to follow some procedure that generated the work itself. Today, such processes are most often associated with time-based art in which the generation of images is seen as a progression over time. In my generative art the algorithmic element is normally dealt with by using declarative programming, often logic programming to be more specific. Whilst procedural programs describe a sequence of actions to be taken by the computer one after the other, declarative programs describe what is required in terms of rules and it is left to the computer system to work out the order in which things should be done. Thus in making such generative works I do not 'paint' each

Fig. 2 *Shaping Form*, Ernest Edmonds, 2015

image that the audience will see. Rather, I specify the rules that will be used by the computer to perform that task. Many of my works go further than being generative in that they are also interactive, being influenced by data taken from cameras or microphones.

Fig. 3 *Shaping Space*, Ernest Edmonds, 2012

The Semiotic Challenge

Following the public discussion at Oi Futuro, Clarisse Sieckenius de Souza posed the following challenging questions:

> "I thought I would accept your invitation to follow up on some of the thoughts we shared while we were together in Rio, starting with the question I would have asked at the Oi Futuro panel, if I'd had the chance. It had to do with 'misinterpreting' code representations and/or being surprised by unexpected results (one lady in the audience asked a related question, but I have a slightly different view).

I have been recently reading a book on sculpture (Le Normand-Romain & Haudiquet, 2001). From a semiotic perspective, it's intriguing to think of Rodin's Bourgeois de Calais, for example, as ONE piece of work. I've seen "it" in different places around the world (Stanford and Paris, for example). The original clay model was used to produce the big bronze versions. But Rodin "manipulated" (created?) originally the clay, not the bronze. The clay model was, apparently, the manifestation of his art conception. All the subsequent bronze replicas were iconic signs (?) of this primordial representation.

Now let's switch to digital art. Your 'code' is your 'clay' (?) in that it is the matrix of your art and the representation of your conception.

Except...

-- that whereas Rodin's clay model can replicate infinite facsimile copies that are perceptually identical to each other (I recognize the *Bourgeois de Calais* in all instances), your code model generates infinite instances of art that may or may not be facsimile copies of each other.

All depends on what your program does.

-- that whereas Rodin could swear on what was or was not a bronze cast of his model, you cannot really do it, can you? If your program generates infinite replicas of a single output, you are in the same situation as Rodin. But if your program generates infinite types of objects, human cognition may not be able to tell whether some instance of digital art is or is not an output of the digital matrix, isn't it? Of course there is a discussion about patterns and meta-patterns, but I suppose that if your program has certain kinds of randomness in it, you might be unable to predict its output. And if I carry this one step further, you might be unable to tell whether your program is the EXACT expression of your conception, because you cannot run it infinite times and tell that, as far as what you mean by your conception, all outputs express exactly what you mean. Can you? There might be a bug in the program. But Rodin can always tell, and I suppose his clay model is guaranteed bug-free.

So, I am intrigued by the 'locus' of art conception, or perhaps the relation between mind, code and matter, if you'll excuse my ignorance of the appropriate terms. Can a single image instance (material) of an infinite set of image instances (immaterial) potentially produced by a program (a textual representation of a mechanical instance-generating procedure) be always legitimately said to have been "created" by the digital artist? I am ready to accept that any one of the potential infinite replicas of the Bourgeois de Calais will have been legitimately "created" by Rodin. I suspect that the finite mind of any human artist has a limit to conception that can be, intentionally or unintentionally, extrapolated by some kinds of programs he or she creates (not all, of course) as a sign of his or her art.

One may bring up the classical semiotic argument that semiosis is infinite and that there are no two identical fruitions of the same piece of art. Yes. However, I am not looking at "fruition" (the receiver's role), but at "recognition of one's own materialized conception" (the sender's role). Can the digital artist always tell whether a piece is his or not? Where does identity lie in this case?

If you've come this far, thank you. You may perhaps recognize some Semiotic Engineering theory hiding in the back of my questioning. You will be right. There is a connection."

In the next section I record my reply.

The Response

This is a complex set of questions. First of all, let us consider the Rodin case. Of-course, we cannot tell what was in his mind, but the question must be put, did he see the original clay model as the manifestation of his art conception? Perhaps, but quite possibly the materiality of bronze was a key feature of that conception and, if that was so, only the first casting could count as the primordial representation. Of-course, we are not able to answer this question, but let us consider for a moment the possibility that the answer is "No" – that the first casting was the first time that his conception was realized. I am not sure that this makes a vital difference to your questions, but clearly it could be that each representation, including the first, is identical. Perhaps in some ways that is easier for us, as I will go on to explain.

The Digital Art Question

So, let us switch to digital art and, in particular, the use of code in my work. Well, first of all, the code is not the art object. The object also has various material features, such as size and texture, as well as behavioural properties: the code is static but the art work that the code "drives" changes in time. This last point is the same issue as arises in a semiotic consideration of the relationship between any code and the relevant running system. So it is not an art question in particular and I am quite sure that you have a clear answer for it.

You suggest that my code is my version of Rodin's clay and, accepting the "No" answer above, I can agree at one level. The code defines many of the key attributes of the final work just as Rodin's clay model defines most aspects of *Bourgeois de Calais*. However, you quite correctly point out a key difference. Yes, all of the instances of this Rodin sculpture are perceptually identical (at least near enough for this argument) whereas the code generates distinguishably different instances. I think this is a key point in your remarks and I will go into some detail in my response.

My code cannot be seen as the full manifestation of my art conception, clearly, but it is further away, one might say, than Rodin's model. Leaving materiality aside, one of the castings is an equivalent instance of the clay model. It is much harder to say something like that in relation to my code. Let us take a few different examples of how it can work, starting with earlier and simpler works than the *Shaping Form/Space* series.

The Generative Art Case

My first computer generated time-based artworks, I called them *Video Constructs*, were completely deterministically generative (Edmonds, 1989). That is, they had a specific starting point and always developed from that point in exactly the same way. Some of them were potentially infinitely long, without repetition, however. So every instance is the same proving that the delivery context, in particular the monitor used, is the same. In that respect, the code can be seen as, basically, equivalent to the clay and any instance of the realized *Video Construct* can be seen as equivalent to one of Rodin's castings. The issue about the potential infinite nature of the work and hence my inability to check it out is something else that we can come back to. For the moment, we can say that, with the *Video Constructs*, I am on the same page as Rodin.

Randomness and Non-Determinacy

You mention an assumption that my work has certain kinds of randomness in it. Well, perhaps, but it depends how one looks at it. As I have mentioned, the *Video Constructs* were fully deterministic and hence, at least in principle, fully predictable. However, as discussed above, the *Shaping Form/Space* series of works analyse information from a camera and use that to modify the generative rules used. The camera points towards the space where we expect the audience and so the presence and movement of audiences influences the artwork's behaviour. Hence that behaviour is not predictable. We could say that it shows a kind of randomness. On the other hand, the ways in which audience movement influences the work is, in itself, completely deterministic. The point is best captured by noting that, whereas the *Video Constructs* are closed systems, the *Shaping Form/Space* works are open systems. To be precise, these later works use non-deterministic rules rather than random ones. From an artist's point of view this is important because so many computer-based artists have used pseudo-random numbers to simulate randomness and my work does none of that.

Now, this distinction may be less important for your questions than to me as the artist because, in either case, the issue of not being able to predict the output applies.

In this context you say, "…you might be unable to tell whether your program is the EXACT expression of your conception…" This is a key issue. Can I tell? Does it matter? Clearly, even in the infinite closed system artworks, but especially in the open system ones, there is no way that I can explicitly review every state that the work might be in. Nor, incidentally, can I review all possible transitions or how the space might turn out in every possible situation. The progress of the works in time is quite as important as any particular image. Consider music as a comparison. The relationships between the sounds and the transitions from one to another "make" the music and are at least equal to the isolated sounds.

Now the issue of not knowing, of the non-determinacy or infinite nature of these works, is certainly problematic. A little art history is relevant. A founding step in the Constructivist art tradition, the discussions of the General Working Group of Objective Analysis in 1921 in Moscow, is significant (Lodder, 1983). This group of artists drew a distinction between 'composition' and 'construction' in making their art. Briefly, *composition* was seen to be about arranging the appearance of an artwork according to relationship rules and *construction* was about making a work according to a plan for its production. They promoted the idea of concentrating on construction. A significant implication was that they were more interested in the process of making than in the appearance of the final object. Although these Russian artists did not make generative art and were working many years before the birth of the computer, they were, in a sense, beginning to let go of their control of the detailed appearance of their works. So what we might say that generative, computer-based, art in this context does have a precedent.

When I compose generative rules and when I write the code for a generative, mostly also interactive, artwork I feel very much in control. I am after all making a very specific and a very clear specification. It is just that I cannot fully review the visual implications and cannot even imagine every possible outcome. Even if my imagination is extremely rich, as you correctly say, perhaps there is a bug. Here, there certainly is a difference with the Rodin case.

I feel confident enough in my code and the process of running tests not to be too concerned about a bug. In years of experience I have not come across one after I released a work. There have been problems sometimes and they have turned out to be physical, a faulty plug, or setup issues, some setting in the operating system was not correct (e.g. a default to close the computer down after X hours was not disabled). I am sure that we could think up comparable problems in making and displaying castings. So bugs do not worry me. However, I am taking an attitude not required of Rodin in accepting that I cannot inspect every future state of my artworks. In practice I actually welcome this situation. The not knowing leads to fresh discoveries and even stimulates the next creative step. As an artist I am pleased if my work surprises me. This leads to the issue of the locus of conception in my art.

The Locus of Conception

What is the locus of conception of the art or, as you nicely put it, "the relation between mind, code and matter"?

First, let me comment on the artistic process. I am not unusual in saying that making a work of art is a process of discovery, a kind of experiment. The purpose is not so much to produce a particular object as to be engaged in a continual discovery and development process. So looking at the final 'material' sets the mind working again and new, or revised, code is written leading to another material outcome and so on.

This comment on process does not change the question, but it helps to explain why an artist might not be so concerned about the possibility of generating an Image instance that they had not expected. In such cases, can the image instances be said to be created by the artist? They are created by the code written by the artist, by me in this case (perhaps I should stress again that I do not use random or pseudo-random elements except in the sense that the works we are concentrating on are open systems). The question seems to relate to the way that we interpret *intention* in this context. Clearly I did not specifically intend my code to generate an image that surprises me, but that image does belong to a class, possibly a class with infinite members, that I did intend it to be a member of. So my intention is to generate images and sequences of images in some given class. The question then is, does it make sense to say that the locus of conception of the art is in the class rather than the instance?

Taking this further, can the recognition of my "materialized conception" be found in the identification of the membership of a class rather than in the accurate replication of something? Identity may lie a layer up from the material. Even in painting something of this kind can occur. Picasso, when asked to sign works that were thought to be his, preferred to consider how much he liked them, how well they fitted into the class of "Picassos", than to look for the literal truth. I quote:

> "When a supposed Picasso fell into the hands of one of his avid collectors, he took it to the artist in order for him to authenticate it in person. Unfortunately, Picasso took one look at it and disowned it. Disappointed, the collector bought another Picasso and showed it to him; this, too, Picasso said was fake. Finally, the collector decided to watch Picasso himself make a painting, so that he could be sure of its authenticity. Unfortunately, Picasso once again declared the painting to be fake once it was in the collector's hands. "But I saw you paint this one with my own eyes," the collector protested. "I can paint a fake Picasso better than anyone," the painter replied, deadpan." (Asher & Beaven, 2011)

To return to my comment about the artist's process, the artist is both sender and receiver, and he or she does not always receive what was sent. Where does the identity lie? It remains an open question largely because the artist's intention, my intention in any case, places the locus of conception slightly away from the particular material realization of the work at any given moment and, in any case, is very deliberately a shifting idea.

Conclusion

This exchange is rather limited in that I have responded to the remarks by Clarisse Sieckenius de Souza quoted above and no reply to my thoughts is included. The chapter poses questions developed from Clarisse's remarks as much as it answers her questions. I am sure that the debate can and will continue in other ways but most of all I hope that the chapter has demonstrated that questions about art posed from a semiotic perspective lead to significant thinking about the very nature of that art and its practice. My thanks to Clarisse, as always, for her careful and penetrating questions.

References

Asher MF, Beaven L (2011) The art museum. Phaidon, London

Edmonds EA (1989) Constructing with computers. Art Monthly, 12, p 129

Edmonds EA (2003) Logics for constructing generative art systems. Digital Creativity 14(1):23–38

Edmonds EA (2007) Shaping forms series (ongoing). In: Jennings P (ed) Speculative data and creative imaginary. National Academy of Sciences, Washington, DC, pp 18–19

Le Normand-Romain A and Haudiquet A (2001) Rodin: The Burghers of Calais, Edition du Musée Rodin

Lodder C (1983) Russian constructivism. Yale University Press, London

An Overview of Semiotic Engineering Epistemic Tools for the Design of Collaborative Systems

Raquel Oliveira Prates

Abstract Semiotic Engineering (2005) is an HCI theory that perceives an interactive system as a computer-mediated communication in which the designer of a system conveys to system users who the system is for, what it can be used for and how to interact with it. Based on this communicative perspective, the theory aims at providing explanation about the phenomena related to the design, evaluation, and use of interactive systems. To do so, Semiotic Engineering draws on *Semiotics* – the discipline that studies signs, significations processes and communication – and makes connections to Computer Science concepts.

Introduction

Within the communicative perspective of Semiotic Engineering, both designers and users are interlocutors of a communicative act, in which the designer is the sender of a message to users. The message is the interface itself, which conveys to users who are the users the system is designed for, what kind of tasks they can perform with the system and how they can interact with the system to achieve their goals. The content of the message can be paraphrased as:

> "Here is my understanding of who you are, what I've learned you want or need to do, in which preferred ways, and why. This is the system that I have therefore designed for you, and this is the way you can or should use it in order to fulfill a range of purposes that fall within this vision." (de Souza 2005; p. 25)

As users interact with the system, they understand the designer's message. Thus, the designer-to-user communication is in fact a meta-communication, since it takes place through the system-user communication. Also, it is unidirectional, since users do not have the opportunity to talk back to designers at interaction time.

R.O. Prates (✉)
Universidade Federal de Minas Gerais (UFMG), Belo Horizonte, Brazil
e-mail: rprates@dcc.ufmg.br

S.D.J. Barbosa, K. Breitman (eds.), *Conversations Around Semiotic Engineering*, DOI 10.1007/978-3-319-56291-9_9

In this chapter, we focus on the Semiotic Engineering for collaborative systems. By collaborative systems we mean any system that aims to connect people to interact with each other through the system, be it to communicate, share information or coordinate activities (Grudin and Poltrock 2012), and thus encompasses a range of different systems, such as teleconference systems or social network sites.

In collaborative systems, although the designer's meta-message conveys the same overall decisions presented in the general template, this message becomes more complex since the designer is not communicating with one person at a time, but rather with a group of people (Prates and de Souza 1998). The designer's understanding of *who the users are* may need to consider the different roles they can take in the system, who can take each role, as well as the relationships among them. The definition of what they *want to do* and *how* may differ for each role. Furthermore, the interface must convey the designers' decisions not only about the users and the system, but also about how users can interact with other users through the system. Thus, the designer-to-user message must also transmit who can interact with whom; which codes and protocols are available for them to do so; and what information is available to them about others and their activities. Thus, in collaborative systems the designers' message to each role in the system may be different. Nonetheless, they must be consistent with each other. For instance, designers of a Virtual Learning Environment will have different messages to instructors and students about what they can do in the system, how to interact with it, what they can communicate with other users, and by which means. However, for the system to work well these different messages need to be consistent with each other and create an overall cohesive message about the system.

> Collaborative system meta-message template: "Here is my understanding of **who you are**, what I've learned **you want or need** to do, **in which preferred ways**, and **why**. This is the system that I have therefore designed for you, and this is the way you can or should use it in order to fulfill a range of purposes that fall within this vision. **You can communicate and interact with other users through the system.** To do so, the communication, the system will help you check:
>
> - Who is speaking? To whom? What is the speaker saying? Using which code and medium?
> - Are code and medium appropriate for the situation? Are there alternatives?
> - Is(are) the listener(s) receiving the message? What if not?
> - How can the listener(s) respond to the speaker? Is there recourse if the speaker realizes the listener(s) misunderstood the message? What is it?" (emphasis added) (de Souza 2005; p. 210).

In this chapter, we present our research along the years in supporting designers in the design of their meta-communication for collaborative systems. Thus, in the next section, we present some main Semiotic Engineering concepts that will be important to the understanding of this chapter. The following section presents the EpisTAMiCS architecture models. We then describe the existing models that have been proposed based on EpisTAMiCS. We end with a discussion of the status of the research in this direction, its contributions and next steps.

Some Semiotic Engineering Concepts in a Nutshell

Semiotic Engineering brings designers of interactive systems to the front stage of HCI processes and, ontologically, defines designers and users as equally important (de Souza 2005). By doing so, it aims to contribute to the awareness of what designers are doing and how it impacts users and their interaction with the system.

The designers message to users (i.e. the system's interface) is composed of signs. A *sign* is *anything that means something, in a context or situation, to somebody* (Peirce 1992–1998). Semiotic Engineering classifies the signs present in an interface into three types: *static*, *dynamic,* and *metalinguistic* (de Souza and Leitão 2009; de Souza et al. 2010). *Static* signs are interface signs that are present in the interface at any single moment in time and can be interpreted independently of causal and temporal relations (e.g. buttons, menus, images, etc.).

Dynamic signs are bound to temporal and causal relations of the interface, and can only be interpreted in relation to the interaction and behavior of the interface. For instance, in a text editor, as the user selects a word 'example' and presses the button that represents bold, the text changes to **'example'**. The dynamic sign is the behavior of changing the text to bold format. A dynamic sign usually represents the transition between two states of the system represented by static signs.

Finally, *metalinguistic* signs are interface signs that refer to other interface signs with the goal of explaining the meanings encoded in them. Typically, they are instructions, explanations or tips about other signs. They can be present at the interface level, such as tooltips or instructions, or in another context such as a help system or even a website about the system.

It is interesting to notice that an interface element may have static, dynamic, and metalinguistic signs associated to it. For instance, a button in a toolbar is itself a static sign in the interface. There may be a tooltip or an entry on the help system associated to it, which represent metalinguistic signs that explain it. Its behavior (what the system does when the user presses it) is a dynamic sign that associates two states of the interface represented by static signs.

The designer's activity in creating an interactive system involves deciding and producing the content and expression of the message. Defining the content involves learning or deciding who the target audience of the system is, what goals can be achieved by using it, and how to interact with it (interaction paradigms or principles to be used). Producing the expression of the message involves selecting and combining static, dynamic, and metalinguistic signs. The quality of the designer's message represents the system's *communicability* – that is, whether the system conveys to users the design intents and interactive principles in an organized and resourceful way, which allows them to achieve the intended result (Prates et al. 2000; de Souza and Leitão 2009).

Semiotic Engineering argues that any interactive system is a linguistic intellectual artifact (de Souza 2005 p. 10). A linguistic intellectual artifact is defined as the result of a human intellectual activity that encodes a particular interpretation of a problem, as well as of a particular set of solutions for that problem. The encoding is fundamentally linguistic, which means that it is encoded and can be interpreted based in a set of semantic rules. In order for the artifact to achieve its purpose, its users must understand the linguistic coding system in which it is formulated and be able to explore the available set of solutions proposed by its designer. Interactive systems also require that the linguistic system formulated be computable.

In order to support designers in designing their systems, Semiotic Engineering proposes that there should be tools available to support their intellectual activity. These tools should be *epistemic tools*, that is, tools that do not yield a direct answer to a problem, but support designers in understanding the problem itself, experimenting with different candidate solutions, evaluating the results, and anticipating the implications they may bring about.

In HCI, design models, scenarios, and guidelines can be perceived as epistemic tools, even if they are not framed as such. Nonetheless, the Semiotic Engineering epistemic tools differ from others since they are based on the perspective of the system as meta-communication artifact and support the designer in reflecting upon the system as a communicative act, even if different epistemic tools may focus on different aspects of the message and its design.

In the next section, we briefly present the main steps of a Semiotic Engineering design process, and describe a Semiotic Engineering based architecture model for collaborative systems epistemic tools that support designers in reflecting upon the content of the message they are sending to users.

Collaborative Systems Epistemic Tools

Throughout the years, some epistemic tools have been proposed within the Semiotic Engineering framework (Barbosa and Paula 2003; Silveira et al. 2001; Salgado et al. 2011; Barbosa et al. 2007). Existing epistemic tools have been proposed for different steps of the design process. In designing a communicative act, there are two main activities involved, defining *What to communicate?* (*content*) and *How to communicate it? (expression).*

The first step in defining *What to communicate?* involves making the necessary decisions to fill out the meta-message template[1]. In other words, it involves deciding who the system is for, what they can do, and how to interact with it. The meta-message template itself can be perceived as an epistemic tool, which allows designers to express and reflect upon the overall message they want the system to convey. In the case of the collaborative system template, it may be easier to fill out a template for each role available, but they should be checked against each other to guarantee their cohesiveness.

[1] Notice that, although learning about the users, their needs and contexts would be expected, it is outside the scope of the Semiotic Engineering theory (de Souza and Leitão 2009). Such activities can be performed using known HCI methods, such as direct observation or interviews (Lazar et al. 2010).

Once designers have defined *what to communicate*, they can work on deciding *how to communicate it*. The expression of the message can be thought in terms of the interaction, in which the designer defines the possible system-user communications that can take place to convey the meta-message. To do so, a Modeling Language for Interaction as Communication (MoLIC) has been proposed (Barbosa and Paula 2003; Silva and Barbosa 2007). It was initially proposed for single-user systems, but it has recently been extended for collaborative systems (MoLICC) (Souza and Barbosa 2015; Souza et al. 2016).

In this chapter, we will focus on the epistemic tools aimed at supporting collaborative system designers in defining the content (or a specific part of it) of their meta-message. In this direction, some conceptual models have been proposed that aim at helping designers to focus, make decisions, and reflect upon part of the content of the message that they are defining. Although each proposed model has a different focus, they all stem from an overall support model. We will refer to it as EpisTAMiCS and will present it in the next section.

EpisTAMiCS Architecture Model

EpisTAMiCS stands for **Epis**temic **T**ools **A**rchitecture **M**odel for **C**ollaborative **S**ystems design. It proposes an architecture organizing components which could be useful to the proposal of epistemic tools aimed at supporting reflection on the content of the meta-message. The model is a review of the first architecture model proposed (Prates 1998) and its variants over the years (Barbosa 2006; Pereira Jr. 2016). The model is comprised of five components:

- **Design Language (DL)**: a design language that allows designers to describe (specific) aspects of the collaborative system model being designed. The lexical elements represent a set of dimensions that describe the collaborative system model in some aspect and the set of values each of these dimensions can take. The syntax of the language describes how the lexical elements can be combined and, its semantics, the possible meanings that can be expressed through the language.
- **Interpretive Rules**: a set of interpretive rules that act upon the model created by the designer using the design language. The set of rules identify possible combinations of the lexical elements of the DL and their values that could be problematic in some situations. The set of rules is defined as context-separable and descriptive (as opposed to being prescriptive) (Prates 1998). It is context-separable because the combinations identified do not take into account the actual context for which the system is being designed. It is left to the designers to take the context into consideration as they make decisions about the system. And it is descriptive because the rules should describe to designers the reasons why a specific combination has been identified as a potential problem in order to allow them to decide whether it is in fact an issue for the system being designed and its context, as well as to reflect upon other possibilities.

- **Design Rationale (DR)**: The Design Rationale component stores decisions regarding a model generated by the designer and the underlying reasons for them. Initially the DR component contains the explanation to all interpretive rules available. Whenever the designer complies with an interpretive rule that has pointed to a potential problem, the explanation for the rule represents the reason why the designer has made that decision. Ideally, the designer should be able to add information to the explanation to contextualize it, if necessary. In case the designer decides that a potential problem is not relevant, s/he should also be able to enter the explanation of why that issue is not a problem in that specific context. For a complete DR of a system, designers should be able to associate the rationale for their decisions to the model being created using the DL.
- **Future Scenario Generator**: One of the challenges in collaborative systems is being able to fulfill the needs of different people, different contexts, and even interaction styles among users through the system, as well as how they change over time (Prates et al. 2015a). Therefore, one popular solution is to offer users flexible systems, i.e. systems that may be customized or adapted to users or contexts. In order to do so, designers must define at design time what aspects of the systems can be defined at use time, by whom and how. Ideally, the DL would have lexical elements that allow designers to describe the flexible points of the system. Therefore, the goal of the Future Scenario Generator is to generate, based on the designers' description, the relevant scenarios that may be created by users at use time. This could be interesting for the designer, since the combination of aspects defined as flexible may allow users to create a large number of different scenarios, and they may not be easily anticipated by the designer. Also, by applying the interpretive rules to them, designers could be able to identify any scenarios that may be problematic or undesirable to users.
- **Design Description Interpreter**: Analyzes the model created by the designer using the DL. It identifies lexical or syntactic problems, and also checks if any of the interpretative rules are being broken, and if so points it out to the designer.

Figure 1 depicts the EpisTAMiCS model and how it would be used by a designer. The designer would use the *design language* available to describe (part of) the content of meta-message, in other words, to create a conceptual model of (part of) the collaborative system being proposed. Her/his explanations about the model created would go into the *design rationale* base. If the designer had described any changes that could take place in time in the system, the *future scenario generator* would generate the description in the design language for the (relevant) scenarios that could be created. The *design interpreter* would check the model (description of system and future scenarios). To do so, it would check the lexical and syntactic description of the model, and then apply the *interpretive rules*. In case the rules identified any relevant situation, it would present to the designers the situation identified and the explanation about potential problems or aspects that designers should take into consideration. Designers could then change their models to comply with rules or could enter into the *design rationale* base an explanation why in the context of the system the situation was not a problem. Notice that in Fig. 1 we depicted the

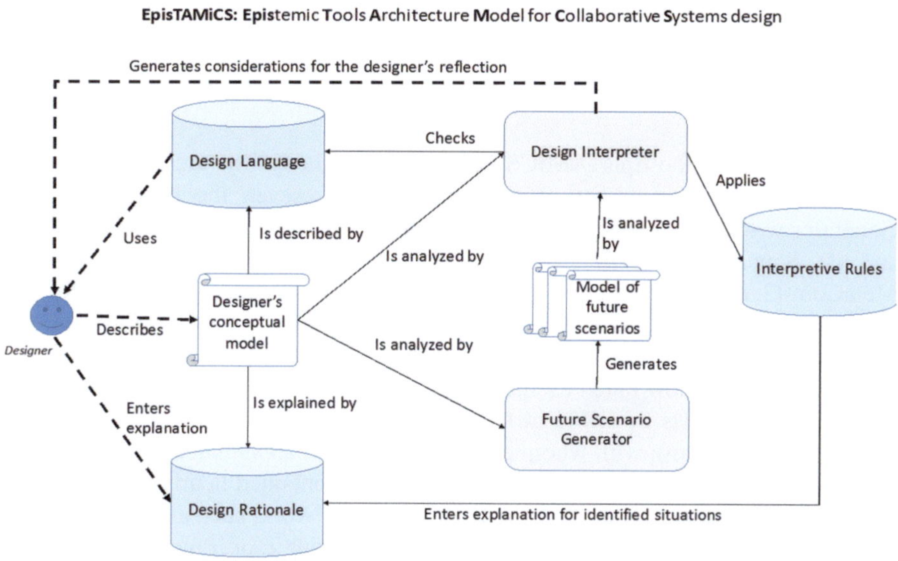

Fig. 1 EpisTAMiCS: Epistemic tools architecture model for collaborative systems design

interactions between the designer and the EpisTAMiCS components using dashed lines.

EpisTAMiCS family models intend to support designers of collaborative systems in two different capacities. The first one is by offering the DL to describe (part of) their meta-message. By doing so, the designer has to reflect upon the dimensions represented in the DL, the possible values they could take, and which one represents their intended solution. Representations in general work as epistemic tools since the definition of what to express and how to do so tend to lead to the identification of aspects that may not have been thoroughly defined yet or that might be inconsistent with other aspects represented. The difference of the Semiotic Engineering epistemic tools is that they are based on the theory and its perspective of the interface as a communicative act, leading the designer to reflect upon it explicitly or implicitly. The second capacity is by offering designers the interpretative set of rules, which can identify points of the model defined that might raise a potential issue, and explaining to designers what these are. This will allow designers to take into account potential aspects that could be problematic in some contexts and to analyze whether it would be the case in the context of the system being developed.

Next we will briefly describe the models that have been proposed within the EpisTAMiCS framework. We will notice that most of them have not defined all the components of the architecture model (yet), but having been conceived within the context of EpisTAMiCS, one may consider their addition in the future.

EpisTAMiCS Family Models

MArq-G

The first model of the EpisTAMiCS family was MArq-G – its architecture model contained all the components described above[2]. However, the Future Scenario Generator was only described theoretically and not instantiated (Prates 1998; Prates and de Souza 1998). The design language in the model was denominated MetaCom-G, and it focused on group models and allowed designers to describe the main features of a groupware system. The lexical elements of the DL described: the *roles* the users can take; the *hierarchical* relation among them; the group's *collaboration model* – i.e. how much each role's activity depended on the activity of other members; the *objects* available in the system, and whether they were private or shared (and by whom); with whom each member could *communicate* and how, and what they could *see* in the system. The set of rules contained heuristics that aimed at identifying situations that could hinder the group's work, such as if users shared an object but could not communicate to each other about it; or if members who collaborated with each other by having to do some activities together did not have any awareness of the other members' activities. The Design Rationale base contained the explanation for the rules and allowed designers to enter an explanation whenever a potential problem was identified which s/he did not consider to be a problem in the context of the system.

Later these models were extended to provide the possibility of a richer description of the communication among group members (Barbosa et al. 2005). The motivation for this extension was that MetaCom-G focused on the collaboration among members based on their activities, whereas in some systems, such as online communities, communication itself was the main activity among members. The new DL, denominated MetaCom-G*, allowed for a more detailed description of the communication among group members. To do so, it exchanged the existing lexical elements that allowed designers to express that there was a communication between members for lexical elements that allowed designers to describe the purpose of the communication based on Searle's Speech Act Theory (Searle 1992) and its structure.

Prototypes to allow for the use of these models (original and extended versions) as epistemic tools were developed in Prolog, and had as interface a command language that implemented the model's design language. Both models underwent preliminary evaluations, conducted mainly by their proponents.

[2] This first model proposed an extra component, which was the Widget Advisor. The goal of the Widget advisor was to suggest possible interface elements, based on the model described. However, this component was later dropped, since the architecture model aimed at supporting designers in defining the content of the meta-message and the widget advisor was an attempt to support the designer in thinking about its expression. Furthermore, the other components focused on an abstract model, whereas the Widget Advisor would be dependent on specific technologies.

Manas

Once Semiotic Engineering was consolidated as a theory (de Souza 2005), there was a new proposal of a model based on EpisTAMiCS, denominated Manas (Barbosa 2006; Barbosa et al. 2007). The goal was that the model would help designers to not only make decisions about the collaborative activity, but also lead them to think explicitly about the design as a communicative act. To achieve this goal, Manas proposed describing any interaction among users through the system as a communicative act among them. Manas' architecture model was based on EpisTAMiCS, except for the Future Scenario Generator, which was not included. The design language proposed, named L-ComUSU, proposed as lexical elements: *interlocutors* (senders and receivers – addressed and not-addressed), the *purpose of the communication* (described by Searle's speech act), its *topic* and *content*. For each of these elements a set of attributes should be defined. Namely, designers should describe if there was an *explicit representation* of the value of the dimension within the system; what its *scope* would be (or value it could take); who would *determine the value* (user or system), if the value should be *mandatory*, and if a *default value* should be assigned. Also, designers should specify what level of processing the system should perform on the information (e.g. just show it, organize it or generate new aggregate data).

Manas's interpretive rules focused on potential social impacts of the systems upon users. Thus, the heuristic rules proposed identified aspects related to social values, such as politeness and privacy. Often the rules would indicate benefits and costs associated to a decision (and not only potential problems). For instance, if the designer decided to explicitly represent in the system the purpose of a communication, Manas would inform her/him that, if on the one hand this decision could provide for a clearer communication intent, but on the other hand it might not be pleasant to the listener or even put the speaker in an awkward position. Another example would be if the designer defined that the system would be responsible for determining who the receivers of a message were, Manas would inform her/him that this could be efficient to maintain communication protocols, but could prevent senders from privately speaking to other users, which might not be desirable.

Manas was evaluated in an analytical context and a review of some of the lexical elements was proposed (da Silva and Prates 2008; da Silva 2009). The review did not introduce any new elements, but proposed changes to some of the existing ones. The main change was to propose that for any user communicative act it would be relevant to be able to represent its attributes for senders and receivers separately (if needed), since they might have a different view of some of the elements of the communicative act. For instance, in sending a message it might be possible for the sender to include not-addressed receivers, of whom the addressed receivers would not be aware. Also, a new attribute was included that allowed designers to specify in which *moment* of the communicative act the element would be explicitly represented (during the definition of the message, or after it had been sent). Furthermore, changes to the set of values of two other dimensions were proposed (explicit representation: to allow for the definition of which type of signs would be used in the representation – metalinguistic, dynamic or static; and values for processing level). A few new rules related to the changes and new issues that might be relevant were added to the original set of rules.

Based on this review, a modeling tool for Manas – SMART (collaborative systems **S**ocial i**M**pacts identific**A**tion suppo**R**t **T**ool) – was developed and made available (Fig. 2 shows some SMART screenshots) (da Silva et al. 2010). The tool allowed other analyses of Manas in a design context (as part of a course's project) (Prates and Silva 2010), as well as other evaluation contexts (da Silva and Prates 2008; Barros and Prates 2014). The main findings of these works were that Manas was useful in designing and evaluating collaborative systems, and supported designers in reflecting upon the system's social impacts. In the design experiment one of the participants commented that by using Manas L-ComUSU, they paid more attention and thought more about social aspects of their design than they had up to that moment. Some participants also reported that some of the explanations about potential problems led them to make changes to their designs. The evaluation of existing systems using Manas allowed evaluators to identify points they considered to be problems and to think about redesign proposals for the system. These works reported that the main cost in using Manas was learning L-ComUSU (what the dimensions meant and their values), as well as the theory and knowledge that was necessary to understand Manas and use it, for instance, how to think about and express activities in the system as communicative acts.

More recently, new models have been proposed with focus on specific problems – one of them focuses on helping designers anticipate possible scenarios resulting from user configurations and the other on privacy in social network sites. In both cases, one point considered was whether they should extend one of the existing models, or should propose yet a new model and design language. In both works, the decision was to propose a new model. The main cost of this decision is having many different models available that do not interact with each other, making it dif-

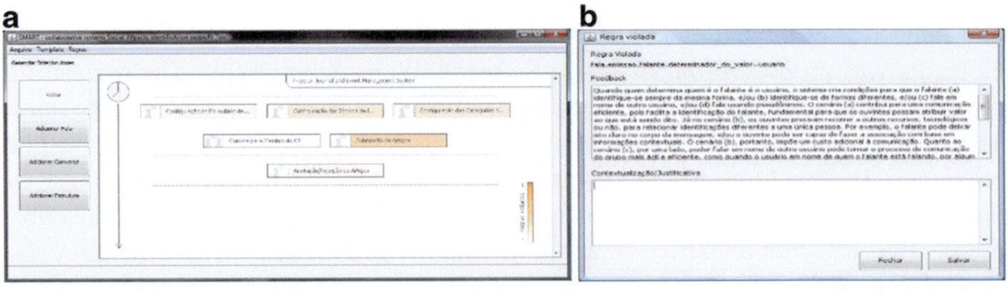

Fig. 2 SMART (Interface in Portuguese). (**a**) Presents each communicative act and how they are structured; the color represents whether there is any feedback regarding the rules associated to that communicative act; (**b**) When a rule is broken, it presents the rule and its explanation to the designer, and allows him/her to include their explanation about the context

ficult to provide a suite that could allow designers to benefit from having learned one, when using the others. Also, in terms of Semiotic Engineering theory, a more cohesive set of models could be more useful in allowing for a broader adoption of the theory and its models. Nonetheless, one aspect that motivated the decision was that the existing models could not easily represent the dimensions identified as relevant. Thus, it would require a large adaptation of the design language, and it could make learning the models, which is costly, even more so. Furthermore, since the focus was very specific, having a more focused model could be more attractive to designers that could be potential users of the models.

SIGMa

Allowing users to customize collaborative systems to their own needs and contexts makes systems more flexible, and allows them to better fulfill users' needs in different situations. In order to allow collaborative systems to be customizable, designers must define, at design time, all the features or parameters that should be flexible, and how users can change them at use time. One of the challenges of designing flexible systems is that designers may not be able to anticipate all the possible scenarios that users may create by changing and combining flexible aspects of the system (Prates et al. 2015a). Thus, designers may inadvertently make it possible for users to generate scenarios that would not be desirable (Pereira Jr. et al. 2014).

In order to support designers in modeling how users' interaction with the system and among themselves through the system could change over time, SIGMa (**S**cenar**I**o **G**enerator **M**odel) was proposed. It was based on EpisTAMiCS, with special focus on the Future Scenario Generator component, that before SIGMa had only been described theoretically, but had not been instantiated in a working prototype. It was decided that a new design language that focused on possible changes would be better to investigate the full potential of such a model[3]. The goal was to create a language that could express well different types of changes that designers may want to make available to users in a concise way. The focus was the *design language* and *future scenario generator*. The *interpretative rules* component was planned to be focused on at a later moment, and only a few rules were identified as a proof of concept.

SIGMa-dl contains as lexical elements: time period, roles, groups, artifacts (unary or composed), ownership, actions, changes, and relations. *Time period* rep-

[3]The alternative would be to use MetaCom-G or Manas L-ComUSU. Although MetaCom-G had the concept of expressing changes over time, they were limited. Furthermore, since MetaCom-G was not being used, there would be no requirement or need to maintain it and try to adapt it. Manas, on the other hand, was more recent and had been used more. However, it did not include the concept of time and changes, and including that would require a large change in the design language and might make it more complex and less usable.

resents a period of time in which context within the system does not change (and not a chronological time). *Roles* describe the roles that users can take in the system, whereas *groups* allows designers to describe a set of behaviors available to a group that includes members of different roles, or a subgroup of members of a role. *Artifacts* describe elements that can be manipulated by users within the system – unary artifacts are a low-level unit that makes sense; whereas composed artifacts are those that combine unary or other composed artifacts. *Ownership* allows designers to define which artifacts are owned by which roles or groups. *Actions* represent the description (conceptual, not as a sequence of steps) of possible actions in the system that different roles or groups can take. Finally, *changes* and *relations* are deeply related. *Changes* describe what possible changes the designers want to make available in the system. There are four types of changes that can be described: role change, change of the time period (or context of the system), changes in an artifact, and changes in the set of actions available. *Relations* are how designers can associate a described change to an action that may trigger it.

To model a system using SIGMa-dl, the designer must define at least one time period and describe the system using the other lexical elements available. The goal of the Scenario Generator component (denominated SIGN) is to allow designers to explore the future scenarios, by simulating which changes may come into effect under which circumstances and analyzing how the context of the system will change in time. A prototype that supports designers in modeling possible changes using SIGMa-dl and exploring possible changes and their impacts on the systems context has been implemented (Fig. 3).

The model has been evaluated in three different aspects. First of all, it was evaluated using the Cognitive Dimensions of Notations (CDN) – a framework that provides a vocabulary that allows for the evaluation of notations (Blackwell and Green 2003). Next, in order to evaluate its expressiveness, SIGMa-dl was used to describe existing systems that allow users to customize aspects of the system – namely Facebook and Google Inactive Account Manager. The goal was to use it to describe real customization possibilities and analyze whether all the systems' possibilities could be described using SIGMa-dl, as well as inspect whether the scenarios generated by SIGN were consistent with the ones that could actually be created in the systems. In special, in a previous work, a problematic scenario for users of Facebook was pointed out (Pereira Jr. et al. 2014), and it was relevant to analyze if it would be correctly generated by SIGN. Finally, SIGMa was evaluated with six system designers who represented its potential users. The evaluation consisted in an activity that involved the analysis of an existing system, and a (partial) modeling of a new system. The results of these evaluations generated positive indicators about SIGMa's expressiveness (there were no aspects or situations of the systems considered in the evaluations that SIGMa-dl could not identify); and its role as an epistemic tool (the use of SIGMa in the analysis and design activities led participants to change their views of the system or on how to design it) (Pereira Jr. 2016).

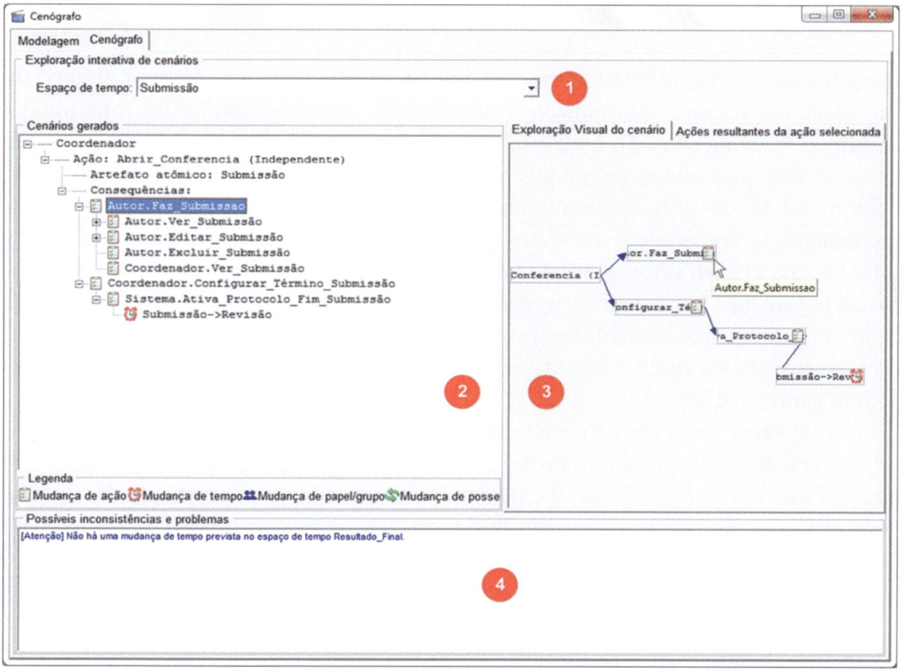

Fig. 3 SIGMa prototype (in Portuguese). There are two tabs, one for modeling and one for the scenario generator (being depicted): (1) indicates the time period being explored; (2) shows the scenario generated for that time period; (3) shows a graphical view of scenarios; (4) shows syntactic or semantic inconsistencies identified

Privacy Design Model (PDM)

The final model that has been based on EpisTAMiCS is the Privacy Design Model (PDM), which focuses on supporting designers in modeling privacy aspects regarding users' communication through social network sites. With the wide adoption of collaborative systems, in special social network sites, privacy became a "hot topic". Although there is a broad corpus of research on privacy, one challenge that remains open is to support designers' in incorporating privacy principles at design time (privacy by design) rather than as an afterthought (Cavoukian 2006).

PDM draws not only on Semiotic Engineering, but also on Altman's theory of privacy (Altman 1975). PDM structures the user-system-user communication based on Semiotic Engineering's design space (Villela and Prates 2015; Villela 2016). Thus, PDM's design language requires the designer to reflect upon user to user communication through the system and their impacts and represent it in terms of: *information source* (who is the sender of the information being shared about an individual[4]); *audience* (who is the receiver of the information being shared);

[4] In this chapter, we refer to the user about whom the information is being shared as *individual*.

communication space (where within the system the individual's information is being disclosed); *individual's information expression* (whether the format in which the information is expressed in the system is predefined by the system or defined by the user); *individual's information content* (defines how personal is the individual's information being shared); *temporal persistence* (defines how long the information being shared is available within the system for). There are also lexical elements that refer to the effects of the communication within the system (e.g. how it may be disseminated by the system or other users): *notification to individual* (describes whether the system informs the individual when other users perform any activities involving his/her information); *speech about the individual* (describes whether the system is able to disclose information about an individual to other users on its own); *information dissemination* (describes whether the audience is able to share an individual's information).

The designer must identify each possible type of user-to-user communication in which personal information can be shared, and then describe it using PDM. For each of the dimensions above, the designer chooses one or more values the dimension can take. For each dimension designers also define who has control over its value, in other words, who can assign its value: if the designer – either at design time or through the system at use time – or the user. If the value of the dimension is left for users to define, designers define at design time the set of possible values that users can assign to it. As of now, PDM contains only the DL component of EpisTAMiCS. There is also available to designers a discussion on how different combinations of values for the dimensions increase or decrease users' privacy in the system (Villela 2016). Nonetheless, this knowledge has not yet been formalized in terms of rules that could be used to compose the *Interpretative Rule* component. An investigation of whether this knowledge could be organized in terms of heuristic rules to be applied on the model created by the designer is a future step of the research.

A visual representation of the model has been proposed aimed at providing designers with an overview of the different privacy dimensions related to a possible communication type between users. Based on this visual representation a tool – PryMeVis[5] (**PR**ivac**Y** design **M**odel **Vis**ualization) – has been developed to support the use of PDM (Villela et al. 2016) (see Fig. 4). The visual representation depicts a honeycomb and each PDM dimension is shown as a hexagon. PryMeVis requires designers to define the relevant communication types in the system and for each one of them to define the value to be assigned to each dimension, as well as determining who controls it. The hexagons are filled with a color that is related to the possible set of values – the darker the color, the higher the level of privacy assigned to the dimension. Figure 4 shows a screenshot of PryMeVis of a communication type described by the designer.

An initial evaluation of PDM was performed with the goal to collect qualitative indicators on the PDM DL's expressivity (Villela 2016; Villela and Prates 2016). In that direction, two aspects were of interest: (1) whether PDM was able to describe

[5] Available at: http://pensi.dcc.ufmg.br/applications/

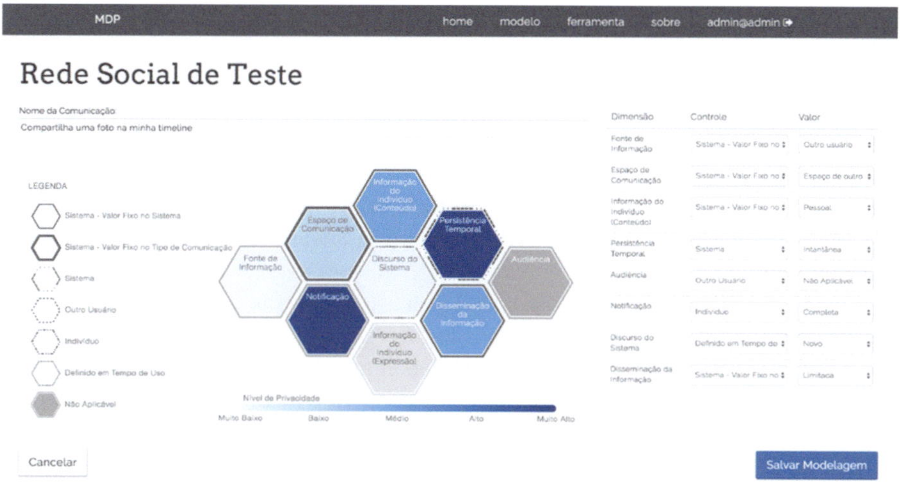

Fig. 4 PryMeVis – Visual tool for PDM modeling (in Portuguese)

privacy decisions in Social Network Sites (SNSs); and (2) whether it could express the differences in the designer's decisions about privacy. In order to explore these issues, PDM was used to describe three different existing SNSs (Facebook, ResearchGate and CaringBridge) and in an analytical activity with potential users of the model. The results indicated that PDM DL could be used to describe the different privacy aspects of the SNSs. Furthermore, through its representation of the design decisions, designers could understand their differences and discuss how different combinations could be more interesting in the distinct contexts – showing its potential as an epistemic tool.

Discussion and Final Remarks

All the models of the EpisTAMiCS family aim at supporting designers in defining part of the content of their collaborative system meta-message. In other words, the goal is to support them in taking into consideration relevant aspects of a collaborative system as they are making decisions about the solution they are going to offer users. The models' design language lead designers to think about the different dimensions and their values and combinations as they use it to describe their solution. The models interpretative rules go further and point designers to situations that could result from their decisions that may be potential problems, and worth considering.

As we have presented, MetaCom-G focuses on an overall description of activities of groups working together, and the impact of the designer decisions may have on the interactions and relations of group members. SIGMa-dl dimensions also allow for the description of group activities (allows for the representation of objects, with whom they are shared and how), but focus mainly on allowing designers to describe changes and generating the future scenarios for designers' analyses. SIGMa was motivated by the original MArq-G work and efforts to create systems that can be customized, adapted or extended by users. Even in looking only at customizable systems there are a number of challenges that users face (Pereira Jr. et al. 2014; de Souza et al. 2010; Prates et al. 2015b, 2016), and that designers should consider and anticipate at design time (Prates et al. 2015a). Nonetheless, there is not much work that supports designers in this effort (Wulf and Golombek 2001), and SIGMa is an epistemic tool that may be useful in advancing the state of the art in this direction.

Manas and PDM focus more on social aspects of systems' use. Manas allows for the description of the communication among group members and analyzes (by means of its heuristic rules) the social impacts it may have on users. It is interesting to note that Manas can be used to model systems in which there is no direct communication, by thinking and modeling activities as indirect communicative acts (da Silva and Prates 2008; da Silva 2009). By doing so, it makes the Semiotic Engineering communication perspective explicit to designers and helps them frame their decisions as communicative acts. Although Manas is able to offer some feedback regarding privacy, it does not make explicit to designers which aspects of the communication directly impact users' privacy. As current systems and technologies have made privacy a relevant concern for users and designers, PDM was proposed to support designers in taking privacy into account at design time for social network sites. It frames communication among users in terms of the Semiotic Engineering design space dimensions and associates them to privacy aspects.

Learning a new representation has an associated cost to designers. However, in order for the model to be useful, its benefits need to justify the cost of learning it. Although all the EpisTAMiCS family models have been initially evaluated, most of the assessment performed focused on the expressiveness of the model and identifying whether it could bring benefits as epistemic tools, that is, whether they could lead designers to take into consideration new relevant aspects and situations they had not reflected upon. Models that have a very specific focus, such as SIGMa and PDM, can have their use motivated in contexts in which future scenarios generated by customization and privacy are relevant issues to designers. The downside is that there are fewer opportunities to use the design language learned and even consolidate its understanding, if compared with more general models such as ConcurTaskTrees (CTT) (Paternò 2004) or UML (Rumbaugh et al. 2004). At any rate, they bring a relevant contribution to the investigation on how to deal with these issues at design time.

All the EpisTAMiCS family models advance the research in Semiotic Engineering by investigating tools that can support a design process that is based on the theory, even if they currently only support part of process needed to make decisions and design a meta-communication act. Furthermore, by increasing the number of case studies of systems being designed within a Semiotic Engineering theoretical grounding, we can collect data that in the long term will allow us to discuss how theoretical based models, methods, and approaches can or cannot offer different results than empirical HCI methods.

The next steps in this research involve performing a more extensive evaluation of the models including collecting data on each one's costs and benefits. Also, a direction of interest is investigating how these models can be integrated with other Semiotic Engineering epistemic tools, such as MoLICC. The idea would be not only to combine them in different steps of the process, but rather to explore whether one could facilitate in any capacity the generation of the next one.

References

Altman I (1975) The environment and social behavior: privacy, personal space, territory and crowding. Brooks/Cole Pub. Co

Barbosa CMA (2006) Manas: an epistemic tool to support the design of communication in collaborative systems (in Portuguese). DSc. thesis – Departamento de Informática, Pontifícia Universidade Católica do Rio de Janeiro, Rio de Janeiro

Barbosa SDJ and Paula MG (2003) Designing and evaluating interaction as conversation: a modeling language based on semiotic engineering. International Workshop on Design, Specification, and Verification of Interactive Systems, Springer

Barbosa CMA, Prates RO and de Souza CS (2005) MArq-G*: a semiotic engineering approach for supporting the design of multi-user applications. Proceedings of the 2005 Latin American conference on Human-computer interaction, 128–138

Barbosa CMA, Prates RO and de Souza CS (2007) Identifying potential social impact of collaborative systems at design time. In: Proceedings of INTERACT, Springer, 31–44

Barros EFM, and Prates RO (2014) Uma análise comparativa dos modelos de sistemas colaborativos fundamentados na engenharia semiótica. In: Proceedings of the 13th Brazilian symposium on human factors in computing systems. Sociedade Brasileira de Computação

Blackwell A and Green T (2003) Notational systems – the cognitive dimensions of notations framework. In: HCI models, theories, and frameworks: toward an interdisciplinary science. Morgan Kaufmann

Cavoukian A (2006) Privacy by design the 7 foundational principles implementation and mapping of fair information practices

da Silva RF (2009). ManasTool: Uma ferramenta computacional para apoio ao projeto da comunicação entre usuários em sistemas colaborativos. Dissertação de mestrado, Universidade Federal de Minas Gerais

da Silva RF and Prates RO (2008) Avaliação da Manas na identificação de problemas de impacto social: um estudo de caso. In: IHC '08: Proceedings of the VIII Brazilian symposium on human factors in computing systems. Sociedade Brasileira de Computação, pp 70–79

da Silva RF, Prates RO and Salles VJ (2010). Smart: a computational tool for supporting the identification at design time of the social impact of collaborative systems. Anais do Simpósio Brasileiro de Sistemas Colaborativos, pp. 39–46

de Souza CS (2005) The semiotic engineering of human-computer interaction. MIT Press, Cambridge, MA

de Souza CS, Leitão CF (2009) Semiotic engineering methods for scientific research in HCI. Morgan & Claypool, Princeton

de Souza CS, Leitão CF, Prates RO, Amélia Bim S, da Silva EJ (2010) Can inspection methods generate valid new knowledge in HCI? the case of semiotic inspection. Int J Hum Comp Stud 68(1-2):22–40

Grudin J, Poltrock S (2012) CSCW: Computer supported cooperative work. Encyclopedia of human-computer interaction. Aarhus, The Interaction Design Foundation

Lazar J, Feng JH, Hochheiser H (2010) Research methods in human-computer interaction. Wiley, New York
Paternò F (2004) ConcurTaskTrees: an engineered notation for task models. The handbook of task analysis for human-computer interaction, pp 483–503
Peirce, C. (1992–1998). The essential Peirce (Vols. 1 & 2). In N. Houser and C. Kloesel (eds.) The Peirce edition project. Bloomington: Indiana University Press.
Pereira Junior M (2016) Um Modelo para Apoiar Projetistas de Sistemas Colaborativos na Antecipação de Cenários. PhD thesis, Departamento de Ciencia da Computacao, UFMG
Pereira Jr M, Xavier SIR, and Prates RO (2014) Investigating the use of a simulator to support users in anticipating impact of privacy settings in Facebook. In: Proceedings of the 18th ACM international conference on supporting group work, ACM, 63–72. http://doi.org/10.1145/2660398.2660419
Prates RO (1998) The semiotic engineering of multi-user interface languages (in Portuguese). DSc. thesis – Departamento de Informática, Pontifícia Universidade Católica do Rio de Janeiro, Rio de Janeiro
Prates RO and de Souza CS (1998) Towards a semiotic environment for supporting the development of multi-user interfaces. In: Proceedings of international conference on collaboration and technology (CRIWG 1998), 53–67
Prates RO, and Silva RF (2010) Avaliação do uso da Manas como ferramenta epistêmica no projeto de sistemas colaborativos. In: Proceedings of the IX symposium on human factors in computing systems. Brazilian Computer Society
Prates RO, de Souza CS, Barbosa SDJ (2000) A method for evaluating the communicability of user interfaces. ACM Interac 7(1):31–38
Prates RO, Rosson MB, de Souza CS (2015a) Interaction anticipation: communicating impacts of groupware configuration settings to users. End-user development, Springer, 192–197
Prates RO, Rosson MB, de Souza CS (2015b) Making decisions about digital legacy with Google's inactive account manager. In: Proceedings of INTERACT 2015, 6 pp
Prates RO, Rosson MB, de Souza CS (2016) Analysis of configuration decision space over time: the Google inactive manager account case. In: Proceedings of XV Brazilian symposium on human factors in computer systems (IHC 2016), Sociedade Brasileira de Computação
Rumbaugh J, Jacobson I, Booch G (2004) The unified modeling language reference manual, Pearson Higher Education
Salgado LCC, de Souza CS, Leitão CF (2011). On the epistemic nature of cultural viewpoint metaphors. In: Proceedings of the 10th Brazilian symposium on human factors in computing systems and the 5th Latin American conference on human-computer interaction, Brazilian Computer Society, 23–32
Searle JR (1992) Conversation reconsidered. In: Parret H, Verschueren J (eds) (on) Searle on conversation. John Benjamins, Amsterdam, pp 137–148
Silva BS, Barbosa SDJ (2007) Designing human-computer interaction with MoLIC diagrams – a practical guide. In: Monografias em Ciência da Computação. Rio de Janeiro, PUC-Rio
Silveira MS, de Souza CS, Barbosa SDJ (2001) Semiotic engineering contributions for designing online help systems. In: Proceedings of the 19th annual international conference on computer documentation. ACM
Souza LG, Barbosa SDJ (2015) Extending MoLIC for collaborative systems design. In: Proceedings of the 17th HCI international conference. Springer, Los Angeles, pp 271–282
Souza LG, Barbosa SDJ, Fuks H (2016) Evaluating the expressiveness of MoLICC to model the HCI of collaborative systems. In: International conference of design, user experience, and usability. Springer
Villela MLB (2016). Um Modelo de Design de Privacidade para o Compartilhamento de Informacoes Pessoais em Redes Sociais Online. PhD thesis, Departamento de Ciencia da Computacao, UFMG
Villela MLB, Prates RO (2015) Supporting designer in modeling privacy for social network sites. In: Proceedings of XIV Brazilian symposium on human factors in computer systems (IHC 2015), Sociedade Brasileira de Computação, 113–122

Villela MLB, Prates RO (2016) Privacy design model for social network sites. 27 p (Submitted)
Villela MLB, Ferreira LS, Barros DAdF, Prates RO, Melo-Minardi, RCD (2016) PryMeVis: Uma ferramenta para modelagem de design de privacidade. In: Proceedings of XIII Brazilian Symposium of Collaborative Systems (SBSC 2016), Porto Alegre – RS. Sociedade Brasileira de Computação
Volker Wulf, Björn Golombek (2001) Exploration environments: concept and empirical evaluation, Proceedings of the 2001 International ACM SIGGROUP Conference on Supporting Group Work, September 30-October 03, 2001, Boulder, Colorado. doi:10.1145/500286.500304

Semiotic Engineering as a Reflexive, Transdisciplinary and Humanistic Theory in and Beyond HCI

Carla Leitão

Abstract Since the early 1990's Semiotic Engineering has evolved from a semiotic-based approach to user interface languages design to a comprehensive theory of Human-Computer-Interaction (HCI). More recently, in 2016, Semiotic Engineering went beyond HCI and gave initial contributions to the field of Human-Centered Computing. This chapter presents three aspects that can be interpreted as constants in the process of permanent evolution of this theory: Reflexivity, Transdisciplinarity, and Humanistic values. The stimulus and support to engagement in critical reasoning about research and practice; the development of a distinct and transdisciplinary object of study examined in light of its own ontology and methodology; and the role of human meanings and values in the theory are discussed as drivers of innovation and transformation. These key factors can serve as supporting analytical categories in discussions around Semiotic Engineering and its contributions, as well as in the learning process of the theory.

A Piece of Conversation

In 2016, the 20th anniversary of Semiotic Engineering Research Group (SERG) motivated moments of happiness and celebration among its members and friends. Additionally, the energy from the strong ties of friendship and scientific collaboration of SERG went beyond those moments and resulted in this initiative: a volume in honor of Clarisse de Souza, founder and leader of the group. In this volume we intend to put in written words what happens all the time at SERG: conversations around Semiotic Engineering.

In my small piece of conversation, I aim at presenting a brief inside viewpoint on the Semiotic Engineering (henceforth SemEng), focusing on what I consider as the most original and relevant aspects of the theory. It is my own speech and vision of the *ongoing* contributions of Clarisse, biased and partial, built to be part of a bigger

C. Leitão (✉)
Semiotic Engineering Research Group, Department of Informatics, Pontifical Catholic University of Rio de Janeiro, Rio de Janeiro, Brazil
e-mail: cfaria@inf.puc-rio.br

S.D.J. Barbosa, K. Breitman (eds.), *Conversations Around Semiotic Engineering*, DOI 10.1007/978-3-319-56291-9_10

scene where some colleagues with different backgrounds and viewpoints discuss SemEng. It is not my intention to choose and describe the main conceptual or methodological contributions of SemEng nor the major impacts of SemEng on the state-of-the-art of HCI and HCC. In this essay I present why I have been drawn to SemEng (and to HCI area) in 2003, what still fascinates me most about this theory, and why these issues may be relevant to the readers.

It is worth mentioning that my perspective on SemEng is an interpretation fully guided by my own trajectory. I am a psychologist, with a Ph.D. in Clinical Psychology and a solid background in qualitative methods, which are consistent with the non-predictive paradigm of science that constitutes the basis of many areas of Clinical Psychology. My Ph.D. research was on the subjective impacts generated on individuals by the diffusion of ICTs. In 2003, due to my Ph.D. studies, I had the opportunity to begin informal studies at SERG and, later, to participate in a research project as a postdoctoral student. Since then, I work as a researcher at SERG, and I have never stopped to study and discuss SemEng.

When I started to study SemEng, in 2003, at SERG, I did not have any knowledge in HCI or Computer Science. At the time, SemEng was being consolidated as an HCI theory, 10 years after the publication of its proposal as a semiotic-applied approach to designing user interface languages (de Souza 1993). The book *'The semiotic engineering of human-computer interaction'* (de Souza 2005a), published in 2005, is the objective benchmark of the birth of SemEng as a semiotic-inspired theory of HCI, with its own ontology, methodology, and epistemology. Thus, I was in a privileged position. I watched the first steps of SemEng as a theory and, as a *foreign spectator*, I was surprised by unexpected aspects of the growth of something really innovative. Initially, I did not have a clear perception of what made this growth an innovative process. I was just experiencing the present time.

Today, after more than a decade, the consolidation of SemEng as an HCI theory is concluded. This time interval allows me to make sense and get the big picture. Now, it became clear that three key aspects of the building of SemEng have fascinated me. They are not particular concepts or methods, although related to some of them. From my point of view, these key aspects are sustained characteristics that work as drivers and enable SemEng advances and innovation in HCI. The first refers to the fact that the theory does not give direct answers to HCI problems. **SemEng is an invitation to reflection.** The second aspect is related to its unit of investigation – the metacommunication dimensions of computer artifacts. SemEng is not an application of semiotic concepts and methods in the context of HCI. Inspired by and based on Semiotics, de Souza went beyond a multi and interdisciplinary approach, to create a proper ontology and methods to study a distinctive unit of investigation. **SemEng is thus a transdisciplinary theory**. The third key aspect is related to the status of the 'human' in the theory. In SemEng, *both* designers and users are interlocutors and meaning producers, influenced by social, cultural, ethical, and psychological issues. **SemEng is a broad humanistic theoretical approach.**

Reflexivity, Transdisciplinarity and Humanistic values have been part of the 20 years of SERG. In 2017, these key aspects seem to be revitalized. SemEng has just begun a new journey. The recent publication of the book *'Software developers as users: Semiotic Investigations in Human-Centered Software Development'* (de Souza et al. 2016) is a new benchmark that gives us evidence that SemEng is going beyond HCI. The book presents recent in-depth research results and the initial contributions of SemEng to Human-Centered Computing (HCC), a field whose object of investigation (still under definition) seeks to articulate technical, cultural, social, and personal factors around the design, development, and use of digital technologies. Again, SemEng researchers are discussing and proposing methods that emphasize reflexive processes. Moreover, SemEng is transforming and expanding its object of investigation in spite of applying its ontology built within HCI to explore more complex problems in HCC. As a consequence, it is not a coincidence that more actors (software developers) are on the stage in a broader humanistic perspective.

In the next sections, the role of reflection, the transdisciplinarity and the humanistic approach are discussed. In doing so I expect that my vision of SemEng can motivate new discussions around the theory, considering that other visions will certainly emphasize other aspects of relevance. I also think that this particular viewpoint can help beginners in SemEng in organizing their learning process of the theory, using those aspects as analytical categories during their classes. Finally, it could be interesting to explore how other theories and approaches are situated in relation to these three aspects.

An Invitation to Reflection

From my perspective, the invitation to a reflexive posture is the most provocative aspect that researchers and professionals have to deal with when getting in touch with SemEng theory and methods. In its formulations, SemEng swims against the tide, as it proposes a set of concepts and tools that should not give direct answers or ready-to-use solutions to research or professional problems (de Souza 2005a; de Souza and Leitão 2009). Influenced by Schön's perspective on reflection (Schön 1983), SemEng proposes to provide conceptual and methodological tools to support reflection. The use of those tools requires time and tough intellectual work. However, some characteristics of the professional industry and of computer science education impose obstacles to these requirements.

Even in earlier periods of HCI history, the software and system development context put pressures that caused some constraints in theoretical and methodological development and application (Carroll 2003). Tight schedules and budgets, standardization and agility are some of them. The following passage by Carroll illustrates the conflict between theory-driven reflection and professional pressures:

> Of course it is important to manage cost-benefit tradeoffs in methods and techniques, to ensure that the benefits expected merit the effort required. But the pressure to simplify has done violence to some theory-based approaches (...) On the one hand, there is enormous demand for researchers to apply and disseminate concepts and techniques. And on the other

> hand, there is little enthusiasm or support for researchers to articulate the relationships among concepts and techniques. An example is the current prevalence – both explicit and implicit – of "quick and dirty" ethnography, but without a comprehensive analysis of the consequences of various ethnographic frameworks. (Carroll 2003, pp. 6–7).

The HCI area tended therefore to produce (and probably it is still the case today) numerous guidelines, patterns, and methods that anticipate problems and provide quick, true-false and replicated solutions to practical problems. These kinds of tools are guided by a predictive paradigm of science, whose methods and techniques have deductive, quantitative, and experimental-inductive basis (Guba and Lincoln 1994). This paradigm is commonly accepted in Computer Science in general, and in HCI as a consequence. Besides, the predictive paradigm of science is dominant in computer science education, considering the algorithmic nature of its object of study.

Science has an alternative paradigm, the non-predictive paradigm, widely spread in social and human sciences, which evokes the impossibility to make predictions, considering the human and social nature of certain types of objects of study (Guba and Lincoln 1994). Taking into account that the object of HCI introduces human factors into the research context, non-predictive paradigms began to be used in HCI by some researchers (de Souza and Leitão 2009). The knowledge produced is from a different nature when compared with those obtained guided by predictive paradigm. It is interpretative and based on meanings. A non-predictive paradigm also introduces different methods to do research – the qualitative methods (Creswell 2009). These methods support reflection and interpretation, aiming at broadening and changing the view of problems and solutions related to a certain object, phenomenon or activity (de Souza and Leitão 2009). Although a non-predictive paradigm gives basis to various research projects in HCI, computer science education traditionally does not give much space for the acquisition of a solid epistemological and methodological qualitative proficiency.

In 2005, de Souza emphasized in the introduction of the first book of SemEng (de Souza 2005a) that the product of her work is a *non-predictive* theory of HCI about meanings and sense-making. She adds:

> (…) there is no room for a purely objective and stable account for meaning (…) [methodological tools proposed by SemEng] must enable researchers to identify the limits of subjectivity, the power of culture determination, the conditions of social contracts in communicative phenomena, and, in the particular domain of HCI, the effects of computer technology upon human signification and communication processes. Sound choices will protect researchers and professional practitioners against adopting a naïve idealized view in which interactive computer-bases artifacts can be built according to laws that are similar to the ones that allow civil engineers to build bridges. (de Souza 2005a, p. 28).

This quote reveals (and motivates) the shift (from predictive to non-predictive paradigm) that those who want to 'start conversations' with SemEng must make. Strongly inspired by Schön's reflection-in-action perspective (Schön 1983), de Souza states that HCI theories should not provide direct and definitive solutions to be inscribed in computational artifacts. From her perspective, HCI problems do not have true and final solutions. Thus, designers must learn to deal with these problems in creative ways.

Still inspired by Schön, de Souza (de Souza 2005a; de Souza and Leitão 2009) considers that SemEng must provide epistemic tools to help professionals in developing reflective, interpretive, and analytical HCI practices. These tools must help designers to learn the nature of the problems and reflect on better way(s) to solve them. The answers are based most frequently on innovation-oriented solutions.

Since 2005, de Souza and SERG researchers have developed a set of epistemic tools aiming to help HCI designers internalize such reflective reasoning. These tools have been proposed to focus on the communicability of interaction design. SemEng offers design tools that support the design of computational interactive discourses by choosing meanings and representations to be inscribed in digital artifacts. The Modeling Language for Interaction as Conversation (MoLIC) (Barbosa and Paula 2003) and the Cultural Perspective Metaphors (CVM) (Salgado et al. 2013) are two examples of design tools. The theory also has epistemic tools for evaluation, such as the Communicability Evaluation Method (CEM) (Prates et al. 2000) and the Semiotic Inspection Method (SIM) (de Souza et al. 2006).

Most of these epistemic tools (except CVM) have been originally designed focusing on "reflective professionals" (Schön 1983), professionals who can be receptive to an invitation to reflection and to be engaged in analytical evaluations of their own work.

In 2009, de Souza and Leitão presented a detailed description and discussion of the applicability of SIM and CEM not only in technical contexts but also in scientific research. Based on this discussion, it is possible to state that the SemEng theory and its epistemic tools are useful in HCI scientific research as well as in professional design and development contexts. The qualitative approach is an alternative to explore innovative framings and interpretations of HCI problems, adding new possibilities to knowledge (de Souza and Leitão 2009).

In 2016, the book *'Software developers as users: Semiotic Investigations in Human-Centered Software Development'* (de Souza et al. 2016) presents a new epistemic tool, the SigniFYI – Signs for your interpretation. This tool goes beyond HCI, and contributes to HCC. SigniFYI is a suite of tools that aims to "uncover meanings inscribed in software, their origins, and consequences" (de Souza et al. 2016, p.1). SignFYI is a tool structured by SemEng concepts and focused on reflection. It allows its users to manipulate software-related materials from software design and development to software experience. SignFYI supports reflection *in* action and *on* action.

Throughout their recent book, de Souza et al. (2006) discuss the role of reflection in software development in general and in SemEng in particular. They go back to the fact that reflection in practice is rare in software development (as in HCI), considering time and other pressures for agility. They also discuss the difficulties involved in *reflecting while acting*, and emphasize that Schön's perspective is mainly centered on reflection *in* action. In the view of SemEng, however, there is a moment for reflection separated from the moment for action. Reflection may occur before or after action. Thus, recently, the invitation to reflection promoted by SemEng presents a little change. It emphasizes *reflection on practice*, promoting critical examination in technical or scientific contexts. Although it takes time, reflection may lead to an in-depth and comprehensive analysis of practical or scientific problems.

Building a Transdisciplinary Object of Investigation in HCI

In 1993, de Souza proposed an approach to designing interface languages (de Souza 1993), inspired by existing semiotic approaches in HCI (e.g. (Andersen 1997; Nadin 1988)). In it, she applied existing semiotic ontologies (at that time, mainly Eco's Semiotics (Eco 1976)) to explore interface languages as resources of communication between designers and users. Like other HCI semiotic-based approaches, the first work in SemEng focuses on the study of signs and signification (object of study of Semiotics) in a specific context, that of human-computer interaction (de Souza 2013). All these approaches view human-computer interaction as a computer-mediated communication in which HCI designers and producers choose and encode interface signs in order to promote user activities.

SemEng became distinct from other semiotic approaches mainly because of two factors. The first is its transdisciplinarity, and the second, related to the first one, regards the unique identity of its unit of investigation, the metacommunication process in HCI.

Initially, SemEng applied the ontology of Semiotics to gain insights on how humans interact with computers and how humans can produce computer interfaces to promote good user experiences. In this *interdisciplinary perspective*, the concepts of an established discipline (Semiotics) are transferred to another field of study (HCI). Semiotics concepts can be used to investigate the computer-mediated communication and many other communicational contexts (media, written discourse, etc.) without transforming its own ontology and methods. In other words, we can understand the semiotic-based interdisciplinary approach to HCI as a *one-direction contribution*, in which HCI reaps important benefits from Semiotics without contributing to or transforming that area.

de Souza went beyond this kind of collaboration between disciplines. From 1993 to 2005, a huge intellectual and theoretical work was done at SERG in order to better understand the hybrid object of study of HCI. Computational discourse and human meanings are both part of this object of investigation. The hybrid nature of this object crosses the boundaries of traditional disciplines and limits the benefits obtained from combining traditional concepts and methods from one traditional discipline to understand a new set of complex phenomena. de Souza faced the challenge and explored this new scenario in order to identify, frame, and define more precisely the nature of the object of investigation of HCI. Therefore, she stopped to use semiotic ontologies and methods to investigate how humans interact with computers and went on to develop SemEng's own ontologies and methods in order to account for this specific set of semiotic phenomena. In 2005, the first comprehensive presentation of SemEng as a theory presents an in-depth description of how semiotic concepts of Eco (1976) and Peirce (1992–1998), along with Schön's epistemology (Schön 1983) of practice and Winograd's Language-Action-Perspective (Winograd 1996), among others, were explored to open space to a new set of *transformed* and *transforming concepts*. Since then, SemEng is no longer an interdisciplinary body of knowledge. In a *transdisciplinary perspective*, de Souza constructed an original theory and methodology with a *narrow* and *precise* focus that is capable to enlighten a distinctive unit of investigation: the process of metacommunication (de Souza 2005a, b, 2013; de Souza and Leitão 2009).

SemEng can only investigate "the nature, the structure, the processes, and the effects of *designer-to-user metacommunication* in the context of interaction between people and computer-based technologies" (de Souza and Leitão 2009, p. 15). Metacommunication is communication about communication, *i.e.* communication about how, when, where and why users can interact (communicate) with the system (de Souza 2005a). The designer chooses and encodes interface signs in order to elaborate this metamessage. By choosing (consciously or unconsciously) a group of signs and by articulating them around a communicative strategy in a unique interface language, the designer encodes his/her intended *meanings* and elaborates a *computer-encoded discourse*. Such discourse is defined as a *one-shot message* (de Souza 2005a) from designer to users. The full set of computer-based conversations is planned beforehand by the designer at design time, and gradually unfolds as the users interact with the system. At interaction time, users engage in a sense-making process (as receivers of the designer's discourse) in order to learn the interface language and to unfold and interpret the designer's metamessage. Although the metacommunication process occurs between designer and users, this kind of conversation is a special case of computer-mediated communication in which designers and users are interlocutors in a very special way. The designer 'talks' with the users by a computer-encoded conversation, fully defined before the conversation (interaction) time, thus limited by his/her anticipation and computational coding skills. The designer 'talks' through the system interface that he/she developed. The system interface represents the designer at interaction time and 'speaks' in his/her name. The interface is the *designer's deputy* in the metacommunication process. In turn, the users 'talk' back by interacting with the system interface, *i.e.* 'talking' with the designer deputy.

The scope of contribution of SemEng to HCI is directly related to its transdisciplinary and distinctive object of study. On the one hand, the scope is narrow, as it focuses exclusively on metacommunicative aspects of interaction design and evaluation. On the other hand, a custom-made ontology and methodology provide an in-depth, innovative, and comprehensive perspective of this kind of problem. Narrow focus allows in-depth understanding of a certain class of things to the detriment of others.

SemEng supports the collection, the organization, and the expression of the metacommunication message, "the set of all computer-encoded conversations that the designer's deputy can have with users at interaction time" (de Souza and Leitão 2009, p. 19). A comprehensive description of the metacommunication process is the main scientific and theoretical goal, and the quality of the communicability of computer artifacts is its aim in technical contexts.

The contribution of SemEng *does not* comprise, however, knowledge about the designer-to-user conversation during requirements elicitation of interaction design. In turn, outside the scope of SemEng, some important *interdisciplinary* accounts of the problem strongly contribute to this subject (Dourish 2001; Kaptelinin and Nardi 2006).

Outside HCI boundaries, Software Engineering and Human-Centered Computing (HCC) used to be out of the scope of SemEng, in light of the state-of-the-art of the theory until 2015. It is worth mentioning, however, that "latent conceptual discourse" (de Souza et al. 2016, p. 14) related to these fields had already been produced as a consequence of research on metacommunication. Recent contributions of SemEng seem to be ingredients of a new cycle of reflection, transformation, and transdisciplinary movement.

Focusing on Both Users and HCI Designers: A Comprehensive Humanistic Aapproach

In general, researchers agree that users are the main actors of HCI and the reason for the existence of HCI as a scientific field. Considering the aim of understanding how people make use of computer artifacts and how to better meet user needs and desires, HCI is often considered the soft and human side of Computer Science. From contributions from User-Centered Design and Cognitive Engineering (Norman 1986) to in-depth studies based on ethnography (Dourish 2001) and Activity Theory (Kaptelinin and Nardi 2006), to give few examples, it is difficult to evaluate the richness of the knowledge about the users as the core of HCI research and practice.

In line with this humanistic view, from a SemEng perspective, the ultimate reason for HCI design is to improve users' life, by meeting their needs and expectations (de Souza and Leitão 2009). However, SemEng *expands* this notion and brings another human actor to the scene: the HCI designer.

The expansion of the humanistic emphasis is clearly illustrated by the title of a work published in 2005: *'Semiotic engineering: bringing designers and user together at interaction time'* (de Souza 2005b). While other theories and approaches focus on what happens on the users' side, SemEng brings designers communicating with users. This shift does not mean that the users are less important than the designers. It means that users and designers have equal status (de Souza 2005a, b).

This approach follows from viewing HCI as a metacommunication process. Interactive artifacts are the result of designers' reasoning, choices, decisions, interpretations, culture, values, and biases. An interface will tell users a message about this 'unique package', and is meant to introduce effects and changes in the users' world (de Souza 2005a, b). The abstract representation of this metamessage (de Souza 2005a) is known as metacommunication template, and states the following:

> Here is my understanding of who you are, what I've learned you want or need to do, in which preferred ways, and why. This is the system that I have therefore designed for you,

> and this is the way you can or should use it in order to fulfill a range of purposes that fall within this vision.

HCI designers define the content, the structure, the language, and the intent of the message, often based on user studies (complementary but not part of SemEng methodology). They are collectively referred by the first person "I" (the designer, the design team), the sender of the message. The receiver, as important as the sender, is referred by the second person "you" (the user, the users) (de Souza 2005a, b; de Souza and Leitão 2009).

The metacommunication template uncovers the fact that the design activity is not a process of mirroring user needs and demands. Actually, it is a communication about *decision making* processes, in which the designer inscribes meanings, professional, personal and cultural views, and presents his/her interpretation about the users' needs and demands. The SemEng template also unveils the fact that HCI design is not neutral. As first persons of a communication process, designers are responsible for the meanings they communicate through the system interface. The metacommunication message has ethical and social values as components.

The metacommunication discourse is an inscription of meanings and, as already quoted, "there is no room for a purely objective and stable account for meaning" (de Souza 2005a, p. 28). Designing in 'first person' is thus a commitment. Consciously or unconsciously, the HCI designer conveys in his/her interactive discourse a particular interpretation of the problem, of who is involved in the problem, and of the solution given to it. The HCI designers use their own lenses to frame the problem and to make their decisions. These lenses include filters acquired in a long-term sociocultural process (Berger and Luckmann 1966). They include their academic and professional background. They also include social and cultural values acquired in more personal contexts. All this content negotiates with those collected about the users' reality. Designing is thus a complex process of meaning negotiation. The designed interface encodes the discourse that summarizes the decisions made.

SemEng humanistic approach stresses the power of subjective, social and cultural values on design process and the need for supporting the reflection on designers' and users' values and needs. SemEng conceptual and methodological tools support designers thinking about themselves and about users, as well as about the potential impacts and consequences of their works on human's life and on society. The metacommunication template (de Souza 2005a), MoLIC (Barbosa and Paula 2003), and the Cultural Perspective Metaphors (CVM) (Salgado et al. 2013) are examples of design tools that support the reasoning at design time. CEM (Prates et al. 2000) and SIM (de Souza et al. 2010) are tools to support reflection on action.

Semiotic Engineering and HCC: Transforming and Expanding the Object of Investigation and Its Interlocutors

The book *'Software developers as users: Semiotic Investigations in Human-Centered Software Development'* (de Souza et al. 2016) presents the first explicit and systematic results of the theory beyond HCI. According to the authors, it is the first presentation of the SemEng vision about bringing together software designers, developers, and users. It has a different research focus, which implies a new invitation to reflection.

The inclusion of software designers and developers represents much more than a new instance of the same class of research problems explored by SemEng as an HCI theory. It involves new kinds of communication processes among different interlocutors. Thus, this new incursion seems to represent a new phase of transformation of SemEng research, in the direction of an investigation of a new complex set of questions related to HCC (Sebe 2010).

The goals of HCC are inherently transdisciplinary. It seeks to integrate different disciplines and it has a new object of study, still not well defined. This object has 'natural' system dimensions, such as psychological, social, and ethical, and artificial systems, such as hardware and software. The motivation of HCC is to articulate the 'natural' and the 'artificial' in the design, development, and use of computational technologies. For this purpose, HCC researchers seek theories that are able to identify and relate disconnected sets of phenomena, from different natures (de Souza et al. 2016).

SemEng's initial steps in this field are based on the vision that its conceptual and methodological HCI tools could support a first exploration of these heterogeneous and complex phenomena. However, the SemEng ontology and methods represented only preliminary scaffolds to face the new challenge. In the long run, the research involves much more than an application of what we used to know as SemEng. It is another step towards transdisciplinarity. de Souza et al. state:

> We now characterize this expansion towards the territory of Software Design and Software Engineering as a passage from HCI to HCC, a move that has inevitably imposed changes to Semiotic Engineering's object of investigation and the methods proposed to support such investigation. (de Souza et al. 2016, p.14).

It is not the intention of this paper to present or discuss in details the recent contributions of SemEng to HCC. Regarding SemEng's recent contributions, it only aims at showing that once examining a new class of phenomena, SemEng researchers sustain the reflection-driven reasoning and its transdisciplinary approach. They avoid simplification and engage in another cycle of transformation and construction. It is a matter of reconstruction of a unit of investigation rather than a case of applying previous knowledge.

Regarding the object of investigation, SemEng investigates human meanings inscribed in software (and not only interface meanings) aiming at providing knowledge to improve "tools, processes, and materials that are used by the entire community involved in software development processes" (de Souza et al. 2016, p. 16).

Guided by these goals, the authors examine the role of artificial codes and notations in the production of software, its nature, its syntax, and semantics (de Souza et al. 2016). They also introduce another layer of the metacommunication process, in which programmers are users. Besides senders of their own message conveyed in their software, they are also users of computer tools that aid them in modeling and programming. So, they are also receivers of metacommunication processes of these tools. There are very interesting and surprising effects of the confluence of these messages propagated to the final software metacommunication. Additionally, the characteristics of the metacommunication of programming supporting tools are very specific, considering that the interlocutors are familiar with the codes and notations involved in the communication.

New dimensions of study also impose new methods and tools capable to support the reflection on new kind of materials (*e.g.* notations and codes). The SigniFYI suite is the contribution that responds to these different demands (de Souza et al. 2016). It presents adaptations of existing SemEng tools (*e.g.* the Semiotic Inspection Method – SIM) and a set of new procedures and tools (de Souza et al. 2016) to promote reflection *in* action and *on* action.

From a humanistic perspective, SemEng research in HCC represents a new expansion. The initiative of contributing to this new field brings more relevance to and focus on ethical, human, and social discussions in light of the SemEng perspective. SemEng brings together users, software designers, and developers, those who are supposed to benefit from technology and those who produce the technology. In doing so, SemEng frames software as an inscription of human meanings and software development as self-expression. Therefore, there is no place anymore to the still persistent idea of the neutrality of technology. Its producers are authors and have responsibilities as they inscribe – consciously or not – values on the products they built.

SemEng helps to unveil the ethical responsibility of each participant of the process of digital technology development, and the need for reflection about the human consequences generated by it. In turn, it offers conceptual and technical tools that support this reflection and help producers in their own critical analysis of their practices.

Welcoming the Future

Digital technology development is a history of intense and continuous changes, in dramatic speed (Castells 1996). The introduction of technology in new areas and domains of human life, the emergence of new platforms and tools and of new ways to interact with them, and the constant changes in the technology development processes and paradigms are some pieces of a puzzling scenario. In the scientific arena, the intellectual categories that we use to understand this scenario have to follow this metamorphosis because the concepts that helped to understand a specific set of problems hardly works to explain a subsequent state of things. Changes in the object of study impose changes in corresponding ontologies and methods. And it happens fast. Theories are always undergoing a kind of resilience test, seeking to evolve without losing their distinctive characteristics.

Up to now, SemEng seems to be responding to this test. On the one hand, a trace of restlessness motivates changes and the emergence of new interests. On the other hand, a singular identity is being preserved. A transdisciplinary perspective of scientific problems, an unconditional regard to human processes and difficulties and the demand for a constant reflective posture are characteristics that grant resilience to the theory.

It is worth noting the challenge regarding reflection. Reflecting on complex problems (refusing to reuse existing answers and solutions) requires time, while the speed of ongoing transformations claims for agility and flexibility. From a SemEng perspective, although some time and effort are required in reflection, it may lead to innovation and to an articulated and comprehensive analysis of confusing times (de Souza et al. 2016).

Acknowledgments Thank you, Clarisse, for always inspiring us. Thanks to all SERG members for making our group a special place of conversation.

References

Andersen PB (1997) A theory of computer semiotics: semiotic approaches to construction and assessment of computer systems, 2nd edn. Cambridge University Press, Cambridge

Barbosa SDJ, Paula MG (2003) Designing and evaluating interaction as conversation: a modeling language based on semiotic engineering. In: Jorge J, Nunes NJ, Falcão e Cunha J (eds) Interactive systems design, specification, and verification: 10th international workshop, DSV-IS 2003. Madeira Island, Lecture Notes in Computer Science, pp 16–33

Berger PL, Luckmann T (1966) The social construction of reality: a treatise in the sociology of knowledge. Anchor Books, Garden City

Carroll J (2003) HCI models, theories, and frameworks: toward a multidisciplinary science. Carroll JM (ed) Morgan Kaufmann Publishers Inc., San Francisco

Castells M (1996) The rise of the network society: the information age: economy, society, and culture. Wiley-Blackwell, New York

Creswell J (2009) Research design: qualitative, quantitative, and mixed methods approaches. Sage, New York

de Souza CS (1993) The semiotic engineering of user interface languages. International Journal of Man-Machine Studies 39(5):753–773. doi:10.1006/imms.1993.1082

de Souza CS (2005a) The semiotic engineering of human-computer interaction. The MIT Press, Cambridge, MA

de Souza CS (2005b) Semiotic engineering: bringing designers and users together at interaction time. Interact Comput 17(3):317–341. doi:10.1016/j.intcom.2005.01.007

de Souza CS, Leitão CF (2009) Semiotic engineering methods for scientific research in HCI. Morgan and Claypool, San Francisco

de Souza CS, Leitão CF, Prates RO, da Silva EJ (2006) The semiotic inspection method. In Proceedings of VII Brazilian symposium on human factors in computing systems. New York, ACM, pp 148–157. (IHC '06). Available from: http://doi.acm.org/10.1145/1298023.1298044
de Souza CS, Leitão CF, Prates RO, Amélia Bim S, da Silva EJ (2010) Can inspection methods generate valid new knowledge in HCI? The case of semiotic inspection. Int J Hum Comput Stud 68(1–2):22–40. doi:10.1016/j.ijhcs.2009.08.006
de Souza CS (2013) Semiotics and human-computer interaction. In: Soegaard M, Dam RF (eds) The encyclopedia of human-computer interaction, 2nd edn. The Interaction Design Foundation, Aarhus
de Souza CS et al (2016) Software developers as users. Semiotic investigations in human-centered software development. Springer, London
Dourish P (2001) Where the action is: the foundations of embodied interaction. MIT Press, Cambridge, MA
Eco U (1976) A theory of semiotics, vol 217. Indiana University Press, Bloomington
Guba EG, Lincoln YS (1994) Competing paradigms in qualitative research. In: Denzin NK, Lincoln YS (eds) Handbook of qualitative research. Sage, Thousand Oaks, pp 105–117
Kaptelinin V, Nardi B (2006) Acting with technology: activity theory and interaction design. The MIT Press, Cambridge, MA
Nadin M (1988) Interface design: a semiotic paradigm. Semiotica 69(3–4):269–302. doi:10.1515/semi.1988.69.3-4.269
Norman DA (1986) User centered systems design. In: Norman DA, Draper SW (eds), (pp 31–62), Lawrence Erlbaum and Associates, Hillsdale
Peirce CP (1992–1998). The essential Peirce, vols 1 and 2. Indiana. University Press, Bloomington
Prates RO, de Souza CS, Barbosa SDJ (2000) The communicability evaluation method for user interfaces. Interactions 7(1):33–38. doi:10.1145/328595.328608
Salgado LCC, Leitão CF, De SCS (2013) A journey through cultures: metaphors for guiding the design of cross-cultural interactive systems. Springer, London
Schön DA (1983) The reflective practitioner: how professionals think in action. Basic Books, New York
Sebe N (2010) Human-centered computing. In: Nakashima H, Aghajan H, Augusto J (eds) Handbook of ambient intelligence and smart environments. Springer, New York, pp 349–370. http://dx.doi.org/10.1007/978-0-387-93808-0_13
Winograd T (ed) (1996) Bringing design to software. ACM Press/Addison- Wesley, New York/Reading

MIX
Papier aus verantwortungsvollen Quellen
Paper from responsible sources
FSC® C105338

If you have any concerns about our products,
you can contact us on
ProductSafety@springernature.com

In case Publisher is established outside the EU,
the EU authorized representative is:
Springer Nature Customer Service Center GmbH
Europaplatz 3, 69115 Heidelberg, Germany

Printed by Libri Plureos GmbH
in Hamburg, Germany